# DAVID LEAN

## INTERVIEWS

CONVERSATIONS WITH FILMMAKERS SERIES
PETER BRUNETTE, GENERAL EDITOR

# DAVID LEAN
## INTERVIEWS

EDITED BY STEVEN ORGAN

UNIVERSITY PRESS OF MISSISSIPPI / JACKSON

www.upress.state.ms.us

The University Press of Mississippi is a member of the Association of American University Presses.

Manufactured in the United States of America

First printing 2009

∞

Library of Congress Cataloging-in-Publication Data

David Lean : interviews / edited by Steven Organ.
    p. cm. — (Conversations with filmmakers series)
  Includes filmography and index.
  ISBN 978-1-60473-234-4 (cloth : alk. paper)—ISBN 978-1-60473-235-1
(pbk. : alk. paper)  1. Lean, David, 1908–1991—Interviews.  2. Motion
picture producers and directors—Great Britain—Interviews.  I. Organ,
Steven.
  PN1998.3.L43D388 2009
  791.4302'33092—dc22
  [B]                                              2008054929

British Library Cataloging-in-Publication Data available

# CONTENTS

# INTRODUCTION

THERE IS A STORY about David Lean that I always love to tell. I've never been able to determine the veracity of this story, but it is one of those tales that in one small snapshot seems to reveal everything about David Lean. The story as I understand it goes something like this: A film production company was thrown into a panic when their director had turned in a "final cut" that was a mess. It was frightfully boring and much too long. Desperate to salvage their investment, the producers contacted the best editor in the British film industry, David Lean, and asked him to re-edit in the hopes of saving the film. After viewing the film, Lean confidently told them, "I know what to do." Relieved, the producers waited for Lean to work his editing magic and deliver not only a more commercially usable shorter film, but also one that would save their investment. Weeks later Lean triumphantly returned with the film, stating that it was perfect and needed no further changes—it was three minutes longer than the previous cut.

Whether this story is true or not does not matter. It is the type of story that could be true of David Lean and it perfectly illustrates Lean's guiding principle. Films, and the business of filmmaking, should have one common goal: Tell a good story and tell it well. A film's duration—and its impact on financial return—is irrelevant as long as the story is engaging, the film is properly paced, and, most importantly, it does not bore. It was this tenet that was a touchstone for Lean throughout his entire career and produced films that, to this day, continue to intrigue and entertain. Epic films such as *Lawrence of Arabia* and *Doctor Zhivago* remain popular video purchases, and his films consistently find themselves at the top of any Top Ten film list.

Aside from a popular appreciation, Lean was also a gifted craftsman, often straddling that fine line between commercialism and artistry. To view one of

Lean's films is to see the complete spectrum of tools available to a filmmaker—and used to their fullest potential. Like his contemporaries (Michael Powell, Orson Welles, John Ford), Lean understood fully that telling a story cinematically requires several components: a quality script, precision editing, dramatic composition, and structured sound. Nothing was overlooked or neglected.

When he spoke to Kevin Brownlow in 1990, David Lean remarked that "I've never really thought of being a film director. . . . I've always thought this [career was] some sort of luck, trick, fluke that's happened to come my way." While not entirely a stroke of luck, David Lean's destiny would certainly seem unlikely. Lean grew up in Croyden, United Kingdom, to a strict Quaker household. His father was a middle-class accountant who worked a regular nine-to-five schedule and demanded little from life. Lean's younger brother, Edward, was considered the smart one in the family and thus was the focus of most of his father's attention. David was not like the rest of the family. Left alone and with an immense feeling of worthlessness, Lean began to discover other interests that his father saw to be of little value.

It all began with a small Brownie box camera that Lean received as a gift from his uncle. He had an immediate bond with the camera and began to form an appreciation for the visual medium. Though going to the cinema was forbidden, his imagination was sparked by the family's house cleaner who regaled him with stories of Charlie Chaplin, Errol Flynn, and others. It was only after his father sent him, at the age of thirteen, to a Quaker school in Reading that he was able to venture out surreptitiously to the local cinema. The experience was revelatory. Upon seeing his first film, *The Hound of the Baskervilles*, Lean fell in love with movies. As he told *Time* magazine in 1984, "That beam of light traveling through the smoke, it had an immediate magic for me."

Eventually, after being unable to find any enjoyment or success in his father's accounting practice, Lean landed a job as an errand boy at the Gaumont Studios just as the sound era was breaking new ground in the film industry. "By the time I was nineteen," Lean said to Hollis Alpert, "I was spending all my spare time at the movies, and was mad about photography." For most of those working in the studio, it was simply a job, but for Lean it was a place where magic and reality mixed. "I remember going into the camera department . . . (and) going up to an old Bell and Howell camera and saying, 'What has that done?' And they said, *Roses of Picardy*. . . . And I remember touching their camera. I couldn't believe that this was the source of all the magic."

Fascinated as he was with the magic of filmmaking, Lean was also interested in the mechanics of film production. Lean set about mastering this "new language" and became very fluent in its process. He started editing newsreels and learning the artful craft of placing one shot next to another to create visual impact. By the time he was twenty-two years old, his skills and considerable talent elevated him to a position of editing feature films.

Lean quickly rose in the industry, impressing everyone with his ability to cut a film on an editing deck without the need for an audio track. Sound was secondary; it was the images on the screen that mattered. He would eventually be one of the most sought-after—and highly paid—editors in Great Britain and responsible for cutting some of the most important films to emerge from the United Kingdom at that time. (*Pygmalion*, *49th Parallel*, and *Major Barbara* to name just a few.)

In time Lean was offered several opportunities to direct, but he patiently waited for the right project to come his way. *In Which We Serve*, a film written by Noel Coward, was the opening Lean had been waiting for, and he immediately accepted the position of co-director with Coward. Although Coward was signed on to direct, he deplored the job and was relieved to discover in Lean a talented, capable director to handle most of those duties. It was a perfect pairing.

*In Which We Serve* proved to be a critical and financial success. The film was nominated for the Academy Awards for Best Picture and Best Screenplay as well as the New York Film Critics Award and the National Board of Review's Best Film award. It also proved to others that David Lean possessed the skills and talent to transition fully to directing films.

Under the banner of Cineguild—Lean's production company formed with his partners Anthony Havelock-Allan and Ronald Neame—Lean embarked on a string of films that gave him critical and popular success. These included Noel Coward's *Blithe Spirit* and *Brief Encounter*, and adaptations of Dickens's *Oliver Twist* and *Great Expectations*. Moreover, Lean began to put his touches on all aspects of the creative process including co-authoring screenplays, overseeing the editing of the films, and working closely with the cinematography. In short, Lean was establishing himself as a true auteur, responsible for every aspect of a film's presentation. Admittedly, Lean would probably scoff at such a notion, preferring to call himself more of a helpful bystander. As he remarked to Hollis Alpert, "I won't call myself a writer. I do call myself a bit of a constructor, and a fairly good embroiderer." But few would agree with Lean's modest assessment of his role. He was intimately involved in every aspect of the film production and would not begin production until he was pleased with a script. He admitted as much to Brownlow, saying that he would routinely frustrate people with his method of obsessively working on something until he felt it was perfect. "He really is a perfectionist," Katharine Hepburn said to *Time*. "He doesn't care if everyone dies around him, he'll just take the camera, prop up the actor, and get what he wants."

By 1954 Lean, at the age of forty-six, had established himself as a successful film director. He effectively tackled a wide variety of film styles and genres. He also produced popular films that were unique in their content and clearly stamped with his own voice.

His next film, *Summertime*, would continue his streak of commercially successful films. With its beautiful scenery, Venetian canals, bridges, and ancient towers mixed with a small, intimate storyline, the film was a huge audience favorite. The romantic appeal of the film proved to be so popular that tourism in Venice doubled that year.

*Summertime* also furthered a theme that would arise in a number of Lean's films—repressed sexuality. What is even more unique about this study is that Lean's repressed protagonists were mostly woman. Rarely would a film director broach such a subject, but to present it from the female's perspective was even more daring. From the romantic awakenings of Jane Hudson in *Summertime*, to the sexually curious but unquenched passion of Rosy Ryan in *Ryan's Daughter*, Lean projected onto the screen three-dimensional female characters who were caught between the tenuously moral ground of the strictures of society's mores and the uncontrollable passions of the heart.

*Summertime* would also mark the end of David Lean's shooting most of his films in a studio. Lean began to venture out to faraway lands to create his epic dramas. "Everybody asks me why I make large movies," Lean said to Robert Stewart. "I suppose I enjoy doing it (because) I love to travel." Sri Lanka, Morocco, Jordan, Spain, Finland—those locations were Lean's new studio. This wanderlust, however, prevented Lean from ever settling down, instead choosing to live for the next thirty years in a succession of hotels, trains, and ocean liners.

*The Bridge on the River Kwai* was the first film to fully combine Lean's passion for exotic travel and filmmaking. It would also introduce David Lean to Sam Spiegel, a producer with a reputation so ruthless and coldhearted that Katherine Hepburn was known to have called him a "pig in a silk suit." But the relationship worked for Lean. Spiegel was able to make the impossible happen—unique, distant locations and production elements that could be difficult to find (trains, camels, armies). In short, Spiegel was able to deliver. "Sam could produce rabbits out of almost any hat," Lean said to Kevin Brownlow, "and would get things that I wouldn't even dare make the first move towards getting. . . ." In spite of Spiegel's knack for "producing rabbits" he would continuously lie to Lean, often to the detriment of the film. In interviews Lean would frequently grouse at how Spiegel would often cheat him of his proper compensation, but nothing would expose Lean's anger more than when he was forced to cut back his vision for the film. One could cheat

Lean out of money, but to deny him the ability to complete his vision was unforgivable.

The relationship, for better or worse, continued with Lean's most ambitious, personal, and highly regarded film, *Lawrence of Arabia*, which ran close to 222 minutes (with an intermission). The location provided an amazing backdrop to tell the incredible story of T. E. Lawrence. Lean's film captured the desert as no other had ever done: sweeping views that continued for miles, grand shots of hundreds of Bedouins on camels, and, what some told Lean was impossible to photograph, a desert mirage.

Although the visuals in *Lawrence* were its dominant asset, the film would also continue to demonstrate Lean's unparalleled editing skills, the most famous example being the moment when Lawrence blows out a candle and the story jumps to a rising sun in the desert. "In one cut," noted director Steven Spielberg, "he create[d] the entire scope of the Arabian Desert." Perhaps Lean's best use of visual editing would be the rescue of Gasim from the Devil's Anvil. Within seventeen cuts (and highly selective audio), Lean combined three elements—Lawrence on camel, Gasim walking in the desert, and a glowing sun—into one of the film's most dramatic moments. Rarely has a director been able to create a montage of such precision and power within the context of a commercial film. It was a moment true to Lean's philosophy: always tell the story in cinematic terms.

The production of *Lawrence* would also introduce Lean to a writing partner for his next three films, Robert Bolt. Their relationship was intense. Both men would work endlessly on a script until all the elements, dialogue and visual, were perfect. The flow of ideas was often so back-and-forth that, sometimes, Lean would not know which person had suggested a particular shot or edit.

*Lawrence* again proved Lean's ability to produce a commercial success. The film garnered seven Academy Awards including Best Picture, Best Director, and Best Editing. However, the normally positive critical reaction to a David Lean film began to take a huge turn in a surprisingly different direction. No longer was he the director that did small, intimate films about "real" characters; in the critic's eye he was becoming a sell-out with *Lawrence*. The film was not seen for what it was: a complex character study on a wide-canvas. Rather, in the critic's opinion, it was just one more in a series of long, bloated, overly commercial "epic" films (*Cleopatra, El Cid, Fall of the Roman Empire*) that were being churned out of Hollywood to combat the popular rise of television.

The relationship between artist and critic is a complex one, but for David Lean the slightest criticism was a personal attack. "They work as a pack in a curious way," Lean told Brownlow. "It's probably completely unspoken, it's somehow transmitted, it gets into the air, but when they turn on a director . . .

they really go for you and they get their knives out in a terrible way and it's devastating." These attacks continued through *Doctor Zhivago* and culminated with *Ryan's Daughter*.

At the time of *Ryan's Daughter*'s release, Hollywood was once again in transition. Highly stylized, almost dream-like films were being replaced with gritty, more natural films by directors who were more concerned with capturing reality than with strict compositions and meticulous editing. New directors like Robert Altman, John Schlesinger, and Arthur Penn were shaking up the filmmaking world and producing films that bore no resemblance to the work of David Lean. Therefore it is not surprising that when Lean delivered his next picture—an overly romantic, visually poetic view of love in *Ryan's Daughter*—the critics attacked him viciously. After one infamous press screening, David Lean was asked by a critic, "Can you please explain how the man who directed *Brief Encounter* [could] have directed this load of shit you call *Ryan's Daughter?*" The encounter was devastating and, as Lean would later confess, "was one of the most horrible experiences I have ever had." The experience left him completely numb.

Audiences also experiencing a change of appetite stayed away from *Ryan's Daughter*, allowing it to become Lean's worst performing film in years, its revenue barely covering the film's original budget. In the end, Lean walked away from filmmaking. "I didn't want to shoot another film. I thought, 'What the hell am I doing if my work is as bad as all this? I'll do something else.' I didn't make a film for, what, fourteen years? Just didn't make another film. I thought, 'What's the point?'"

While it is true the Lean didn't *release* another film for fourteen years, he certainly was not dormant. There was the highly ambitious attempt to produce *Mutiny on the Bounty* (once again with Robert Bolt), a film to be released as two parts. However, after many years and several false starts, it was eventually shelved due to a lack of financing. There was also a small, rarely seen documentary that Lean directed for New Zealand television on Captains Cook's anchor. But, to the outside world, Lean had retreated and stopped doing what he so dearly loved.

He would emerge again in 1984 with a cover story in *Time*, the headline blaring: "An Old Master's New Triumph." David Lean was releasing his next film, *A Passage to India*, and the critics were working overtime to make amends for the past. His final film would prove to be huge critical success, receiving notices that even Lean could not have hoped for. "A wonderfully provocative tale," praised the *New York Times*. "David Lean has made . . . one of the greatest screen adaptations I have ever seen," claimed Robert Ebert. And, "David Lean has succeeded to a great degree," according to *Variety*.

The success of *A Passage to India* would begin a renewed interest in the work of David Lean. No longer considered a "sell-out" he found his work being discovered and appreciated by younger filmmakers and film scholars. This appreciation would be furthered by a restoration in 1989 of *Lawrence of Arabia*, a film that had been drastically edited down by Sam Spiegel for television viewing. The restoration of *Lawrence* brought the film to a new generation of filmgoers eager to discover the experience of an epic film on a large screen.

Eventually, this appreciation for Lean would climax with the American Film Institute's Life Achievement Award in 1990. Lean, appearing old and unable to stand, eschewed the traditional "thank you" speech and spoke from his heart. Disappointed by the influx of "sequels" that were being released, Lean beseeched the crowd of Hollywood filmmakers to produce original work. To not, as he frequently quoted Noel Coward, "come out the same hole." He also pleaded with the "money people" to support the new crop of film artists. "I think the time has come," Lean said, "where the money-people can afford to lose a little money by taking risks with these new filmmakers." True to form, Lean angered several in the crowd—especially those who were planning on financing his next project—but he was being genuine to his beliefs and his unwavering commitment to the power of cinema. For Lean, there was nothing greater than film, no matter the cost, no matter the effort to make it perfect—even if it was longer by three minutes.

As is customary with all books in this series, the interviews herein appear chronologically and have not been substantially edited from the form of their initial publication. Consequently the reader will at times encounter repetitions of both questions and answers. I believe that the consistency or inconsistency shown through that repetition will prove valuable to the reader. Moreover, because these interviews have been collected from all over the world, the reader will notice a difference in spelling to reflect both the English and American vernacular.

I am forever indebted to the many people who helped enormously with this book.

It would have been impossible for me to even begin this work without the extraordinary support of Kevin Brownlow. He patiently answered every one of my questions, pointed me in the right direction, and provided unexpected access (and trust) to his interviews with David Lean. I am also grateful to the many writers with whom I spoke that offered their amazing stories about Mr. Lean, offered feedback and encouragement, and made me feel a part of their community—especially Robert Stewart, Mike Cohn, Gene D. Philips, and Roy Frumkes.

I must also give a huge thanks to my research assistant, Marian Breeze, who came to the rescue at just the right moment with an overabundance of energy, intellect, and enthusiasm. This book would never have reached the finish line if not for her.

Closer to home, I would be remiss if I also didn't express my gratitude to Louis Castelli, Ph.D, for his imaginative mind, continued support, and frequent phone calls to various French publications. He graciously passed the torch to me many years ago, and I am forever in his debt.

My gratitude also extends to the David Lean Estate, specifically Lean's attorney, Anthony Reeves, who was incredibly helpful at every step in this process. Also, I must acknowledge the last-minute linguistic talents of Sargon de Jesus and Antoine Larpin, who were invaluable in translating the French-language articles.

An enormous "Thank You" must go to my editor, Walter Biggins. Aside from a degree of patience that continues to astonish me, he never seemed to waver in his support for this project and made working on this book a valuable and pleasant experience. My thanks also extend to the rest of the staff at the University Press of Mississippi who gave me this incredible opportunity.

And, lastly, I must thank my wife, Susanne Lynch. She continues to be my best friend, my greatest supporter, and a person for whom I am fortunate enough to continue to share a lifetime of adventures. I dedicate this work to her.

SO

# CHRONOLOGY

1908    Born March 25, Croyden, Greater London, to Francis William le Blount Lean and the former Helena Tangye.

1911    Edward Tangye Lean, Lean's brother, is born.

1920    From his uncle, Lean receives Kodak Box Brownie, which he uses to take photographs of the family trips abroad.

1927    At nineteen joins his father's accounting firm, Viney, Price, and Goodyear, as a chartered accountant. He is not very successful or happy. Convinces his father to allow him to apprentice at Gaumont Studios at Lime Grove in Shephard's Bush.

1930    Lean edits his first film, *The Night Porter*. Marries Isabel Lean, his first cousin, who gives birth to their son, Peter David Tangye Lean.

1931    At the invitation of Keith Ayling, Lean signs on to work at Movietone News.

1932    Begins working at the British-Dominion Studios at Elstree. Leaves his wife and son.

1935    Edits the film *Escape Me Never*.

1938    Edits film adaptation of *Pygmalion*.

1940    Marries actress Kay Walsh who will appear in a number of his films.

1941    Edits *Major Barbara* and *49th Parallel*. The latter is nominated for an Academy Award for Best Picture.

1942    Directs first film, *In Which We Serve*, with Noel Coward. Film is released to critical success. Academy Award nominations include Best Picture and Best Original Screenplay.

1944    Launches Cineguild with Ronald Neame and Anthony Havelock-Allan. Company produces many of Lean's early works. *This Happy Breed* is released.

1945    *Blithe Spirit* is released and wins that year's "Best Effects" Academy Award.

1945    *Brief Encounter* is released and becomes Lean's most financially and critically successful film. Awards include Grand Prize at the Cannes film festival as well as nominations for Best Picture and Best Director Academy Awards.

1946    Lean's first adaptation of a Charles Dickens classic is released. *Great Expectations* continues Lean's directorial successes, winning multiple awards and nominations.

1947    The second adaptation of a Dickens novel, *Oliver Twist*, is released. Lean is appointed first chairman of the British Academy of Film and Television Arts (BAFTA).

1949    *The Passionate Friends* is released. Divorces Kay Walsh. Marries Ann Todd.

1950    *Madeline* is released starring Ann Todd.

1952    *The Sound Barrier* is released in the United States (*Breaking Through the Sound Barrier* in United Kingdom). The National Board of Review (U.S.) awards Best Director to Lean.

1954    Lean directs his first international star, Charles Laughton, in *Hobson's Choice*. Though the notices are positive, Laughton is criticized for his "over the top" performance. Lean's marriage to Ann Todd abruptly ends.

1955    *Summertime* (*Summer Madness* in the United Kingdom) is released to enormous critical and financial success, and is responsible for a huge increase in tourism to Venice. Lean begins production on *The Wind Cannot Read*.

1956    Due to the death of producer Alex Korda, production on *The Wind Cannot Read* ends. Lean begins production on *The Bridge on the River Kwai*.

1957    *The Bridge on the River Kwai* is released after nearly seven months of filming. The film garners eight Academy Awards, including Best Picture, Best Director, and Best Actor. The National Board of Review (U.S.) also names the film one of the "Ten Best Films of the Year."

1958    Lean begins initial production on *Ghandi*. The film is to be written by Emeric Pressburger, star Alec Guinness, and be produced by Sam Spiegel. The project is eventually abandoned due to Lean's dissatisfaction with the script.

1960    Production on *Lawrence of Arabia* begins. Marries Leila Matkar.

1962    *Lawrence of Arabia* is released with a running time of 222 minutes. The Royal Premiere is held at the Odean with the Queen and the Duke of Edinburgh in attendance.

1963    At the urging of George Stevens, Lean agrees to help the beleaguered production of *The Greatest Story Ever Told* by directing several of King Herod's scenes. Begins production on *Doctor Zhivago*.

1965    *Doctor Zhivago* opens to mediocre reviews but proves to be a hit with audiences, eventually grossing over $200 million worldwide.

1970    *Ryan's Daughter* is released after twelve months of production followed by six months of editing. The reviews are mostly negative and poor box office receipts are poor. Lean will not release another film for fourteen years.

1977    Along with writer Robert Bolt, Lean begins production on two separate but continuous epics: *The Law Breakers* and *The Long Arm*, a retelling of the Captain Bligh mutiny story. Due to the increasing budget, Warner Bros. eventually pulls out forcing Lean to walk away from the project.

1978    Lean directs the mini-documentary *Lost and Found: The Story of an Anchor*. Divorces Leila Matka.

1981    Marries Sandra Hotz after a seventeen-year affair.

1983    *A Passage to India* begins principle photography. It is Lean's sixteenth and final film.

1984    *A Passage to India* is released to universal acclaim. On June 18, he is knighted and becomes Sir David Lean. His marriage to Sandra Hotz ends.

1988    The restored version of *Lawrence of Arabia* is released. At Lean's discretion, the film is trimmed to 218 minutes.

1990    The Lifetime Achievement Award from the American Film Institute is presented to David Lean. Lean begins work on his next feature, an adaptation of Joseph Conrad's *Nostromo*. Lean marries Sandra Cooke.

1991    David Lean dies on April 16 following a bout with double pneumonia. The Nation Film Preservation Board adds *Lawrence of Arabia* to its list of films that are deemed "culturally, historically, or esthetically important."

1999    The British Film Institute releases the "100 Favorite British Films of the 20th Century" with *Brief Encounter, Lawrence of Arabia*, and *Bridge on the River Kwai* listed in the top fifteen.

# FILMOGRAPHY

## *As Director:*

1942
IN WHICH WE SERVE
Production Company: Two Cities Films
Producer: Noel Coward
Associate Producer: Anthony Havelock-Allan
Directors: Noel Coward and **David Lean**
Screenplay: Noel Coward
Photography: Ronald Neame
Camera Operator: Guy Greene
Art Director: David Rawnsley
Editor: Thelma Myers
Sound: C. C. Stevens
Re-recording: Desmond Dew
Unit Manager: Michael Anderson
Production Manager: Sidney Streeter
Music: Noel Coward
Cast: Noel Coward (Captain E. V. Kinross), John Mills (Ordinary Seaman Blake), Bernard Miles (Chief Petty Officer Hardy), Celia Johnson (Mrs. Kinross), Joyce Carey (Mrs. Hardy), Kay Walsh (Freda Lewis), Richard Attenborough (Ordinary Seaman)
Running Time: 113 minutes
Distribution: British Lion (G.B.); United Artist (U.S.)

1944
THIS HAPPY BREED
Production Company: Two Cities Films
In Charge of Production: Anthony Havelock-Allan

Producer: Noel Coward
Director: **David Lean**
Screenplay: Noel Coward, from his own play
Adaptation: **David Lean**, Ronald Neame, Anthony Havelock-Allan
Photography: Ronald Neame (Technicolor)
Camera Operator: Guy Greene
Art Director: C. P. Norman
Editor: Jack Harris
Sound: C. C. Stevens, John Cook, Desmond Drew
Musical Director: Muir Mathieson (London Symphony)
Assistant Director: George Pollock
Production Manager: Ken Horne and Jack Martin
Dress Supervisor: Hilda Collins
Make-up: Tony Sforzini
Hair Dressing: Vivienne Walker
Special Effects: Percy Day
Cast: Celia Johnson (Ethel Gibbons), John Mills (Billy Mitchell), Kay Walsh
(Queenie)
Running Time: 111 minutes
Distribution: Eagle-Lion Gaumont (U.K.); Universal International (U.S.)

1945
BLITHE SPIRIT
Production Company: Two Cities Films
Associate Producer: Anthony Havelock-Allan
Director: **David Lean**
Assistant Director: George Pollock
Screenplay: Noel Coward, from his own play
Adaptation: **David Lean**, Ronald Neame, Anthony Havelock-Allan
Photography: Ronald Neame (Technicolor)
Camera Operator: W. McLeod
Special Effects: Tom Howard
Color Directors: Natalie Kalmus, Joan Bridge
Art Director: C. P. Norman
Editor: Jack Harris
Sound: John Cooke
Re-recording: Desmond Dew
Music: Richard Addinsell
Conductor: Muir Mathieson (London Symphony)

Unit Managers: Norman Spencer & S. S. Streeter
Costumes: Rahvia
Cast: Rex Harrison (Charles Condomine), Constance Cummings (Ruth
Condomine), Kay Hammond (Elvira Condomine), Margaret Rutherford
(Madame Arcati), Hugh Wakefield (Dr. George Bradman), Joyce Carey (Violet
Bradman), Jacqueline Clarke (Edith)
Running Time: 96 minutes
Distribution: General Films Distributors (U.K.); United Artist (U.S.)

BRIEF ENCOUNTER
Production Company: Cineguild
In charge of Production: Anthony Havelock-Allan and Ronald Neame
Director: **David Lean**
Screenplay: **David Lean**, Ronald Neame, Anthony Havelock-Allan, based on
the play *Still Life* by Noel Coward
Adaptation: Noel Coward
Assistant Director: George Pollock
Photography: Robert Krasker
Camera Operator: B. Francke
Art Director: L.P. Williams
Editor: Jack Harris
Production Manager: E. Holding
Music: Rachmaninoff's Piano Concerto No. 2
Cast: Celia Johnson (Laura Jesson), Trevor Howard (Dr. Alec Harvey), Cyril
Raymond (Fred Jesson), Stanley Holloway (Albert Godby)
Running Time: 86 minutes
Distribution: Eagle-Lion (G.B.); Universal (U.S.)

1946
GREAT EXPECTATIONS
Production Company: Cineguild, for the J. Arthur Rank Org.
Executive Producer: Anthony Havelock-Allan
Producer: Ronald Neame
Director: **David Lean**
Screenplay: **David Lean**, Ronald Neame, Anthony Havelock-Allan, with Kay
Walsh and Cecil McGivern, from the book by Charles Dickens
Assistant Director: George Pollock
Photography: Guy Greene
Editor: Jack Harris

Production Designer: John Bryan
Art Director: Wilfred Shingleton
Music: Walter Goehr (conductor), Kenneth Pakeman, and G. Linley
Cast: John Mills (Pip), Valerie Hobson (Estella), Bernard Miles (Joe Gargery), Francis L. Sullivan (Mr. Jaggers), Finlay Currie (Abel Magwitch); Martita Hunt (Miss Havisham)
Running Time: 118 minutes
Distribution: General Films Distributors (G.B.); Universal-International (U.S.)

1948
OLIVER TWIST
Production Company: Cineguild, for the J. Arthur Rank Org.
Producer: Ronald Neame
Director: **David Lean**
Assistant Director: George Pollock
Screenplay: **David Lean** and Stanley Haynes, based on the book by Charles Dickens
Photography: Guy Greene
Camera Operator: Oswald Morris
Production Designer: John Bryan
Editor: Jack Harris
Costumes: Margaret Furse
Cast: Robert Newton (Bill Sikes), Alec Guinness (Fagin), Kay Walsh (Nancy), Francis L. Sullivan (Mr. Bumble), Henry Stephenson (Mr. Brownlow), Mary Clare (Mrs. Corney), John Howard Davies (Oliver Twist), Josephine Stuart (Oliver's mother)
Running Time: 116 minutes; 104 minutes (U.S. release)
Distribution: Eagle Lion (G.B.); United Artist (U.S)

1949
THE PASSIONATE FRIENDS
Production Company: Cineguild for J. Arthur Rank Org.
Producer: Ronald Neame
Director: **David Lean**
Assistant Director: George Pollock
Screenplay: Eric Ambler, based on the novel by H. G. Wells
Adaptation: **David Lean** and Stanley Haynes
Photography: Guy Greene
Camera Operator: Oswald Morris
Production Designer: John Bryan

Assistant Art Director: T. Hopewell-Ash
Set Decorator: Claude Manusey
Editors: Jack Harris and Geoffrey Foot
Costumes: Margaret Furse
Music: Richard Addinsell
Cast: Ann Todd (Mary Justin), Claude Rains (Howard Justin), Trevor Howard
(Prof. Steven Stratton), Isabel Dean (Pat Stratton), Betty Ann Davies (Miss
Layton)
Running Time: 91 minutes
Distribution: General Film Distributors (G.B.); Universal International
(U.S.)

1950
MADELEINE
Production Company: A David Lean film for Cineguild
Producer: Stanley Haynes
Director: **David Lean**
Assistant Director: George Pollock
Screenplay: Stanley Haynes and Nicholas Phipps
Photography: Guy Greene
Sets: John Bryan
Costumes: Margaret Furse
Editor: Geoffrey Foot
Production Manager: Norman Spencer
Music: William Alwyn
Conductor: Muir Mathieson
Cast: Ann Todd (Madeleine Smith), Ivan Desny (Emile L'Anglier), Norman
Wooland (William Minnoch), Leslie Banks (James Smith), Barbara Everest
(Mrs. Smith), Susan Stranks (Janet Smith), Patricia Raine (Bessie Smith),
Elizabeth Sellars (Christina Hackett)
Running Time: 114 minutes
Distribution: General Films Distributors (G.B.); Walter Reade and Universal
International (U.S.)

1952
THE SOUND BARRIER
Production Company: London Films
Producer: **David Lean**
Associate Producer: Norman Spencer
Director: **David Lean**

Screenplay: Terence Rattigan
Photography: Jack Hildyard
Editor: Geofrey Foot
Set Designer: Vincent Korda
Art Directors: Joseph Bato, John Hawkesworth
Music: Malcolm Arnold
Conductor: Muir Mathieson
Cast: Ralph Richardson (John Ridgefield), Ann Todd (Susan Garthwaite),
Nigel Patrick (Tony Garthwaite), John Justin (Philip Peel), Dinah Sheridan
(Jess Peel), Joseph Tomelty (Will Sparks), Denholm Elliott (Christopher
Ridgefield), Jack Allen (Windy Williams)
Running Time: 118 minutes
Distribution: British Lion (G.B.); Lopert Films/United Artist (U.S.)

1954
HOBSON'S CHOICE
Production Company: London Films
Producer: **David Lean**
Associate Producer: Norman Spencer
Director: **David Lean**
Assistant Director: Adrian Pryce-Jones
Screenplay: **David Lean**, Norman Spencer, Wynyard Browne, from the play
by Harold Brighouse
Photography: Jack Hildyard
Camera Operator: Peter Newbrook
Editor: Peter Taylor
Art Director: Wilfred Shingleton
Sound Supervision: John Cox
Sound Recording: Buster Ambler and Red Law
Music: Malcolm Arnold
Conductor: Muir Mathieson
Production Manager: John Palmer
Costumes: John Armstrong, Julia Squire
Make-up: Tony Sforzini, George Partleton
Hair Dressing: Gladys Atkinson
Cast: Charles Laughton (Henry Horatio Hobson), John Mills (Willie
Mossop), Brenda de Banzie (Maggie Hobson), Daphne Anderson (Alice
Hobson), Prunella Scales (Vicky Hobson), Richard Wattis (Albert Prosser),
Derek Blomfield (Freddy Beenstock), Helen Haye (Mrs. Hepworth)

Running Time: 107 minutes
Distribution: British Lion (G.B.); United Artist (U.S)


1955
SUMMERTIME
Production Company: A David Lean Production for London Films with
Lopert Film Production
Producer: Ilya Lopert
Associate Producer: Norman Spencer
Director: **David Lean**
Screenplay: **David Lean** and H. E. Bates, based on the play *The Time of the
Cuckoo* by Arthur Laurents
Photography: Jack Hildyard
Camera Operator: Peter Newbrook
Editor: Peter Taylor
Sound Recording: Peter Handford
Sound Re-recording: John Cox
Production Managers: Raymond Anzarut, Franco Magli
Production Assistant: Robert J. Kingsley
Assistant Directors: Adrian Pryce-Jones, Alberto Cardone
Make-up: Cesare Gamberelli
Hair Dressing: Gracia de Rossi
Music: Alessandro Cicognini
Cast: Katherine Hepburn (Jane Hudson), Rossano Brazzi (Renato de Rossi),
Isa Miranda (Signora Fiorini), Darren McGaven (Eddie Yaeger), Mari Aldon
(Phyl Yaeger), Jane Rose (Mrs. McIlhenny), MacDonald Parke (Mr. McIlhen-
ny), Gaetano Autiero (Mauro)
Running Time: 100 minutes
Distribution: Independent in association with British Lion, United Artist
(U.S.)


1957
THE BRIDGE ON THE RIVER KWAI
Production Company: Horizon Pictures (G.B.)
Producer: Sam Spiegel
Director: **David Lean**
Screenplay: (credited) Pierre Boulle, from his novel; (actual) Michael Wilson,
Carl Foreman
Photography: Jack Hildyard (Cinemascope)

Editor: Peter Taylor
Art Director: Donald M. Ashton
Sound: John Cox and John Mitchell
Music: Malcolm Arnold
Cast: William Holden (Cmdr. Shears), Alec Guinness (Col. Nicholson), Jack
Hawkins (Maj. Warden), Sessue Hayakawa (Col. Saito)
Running Time: 161 minutes
Distribution: Columbia

1962
LAWRENCE OF ARABIA
Production Company: Horizon Pictures (G.B.)
Producer: Sam Spiegel
Director: **David Lean**
Assistant Director: Roy Stevens
Screenplay: Robert Bolt and Michael Wilson
Photography: F. A. Young (65mm Panavision)
2nd Unit Photography: Skeets Kelly, Nicholas Roeg
Camera Operator: Ernest Day
Editor: Anne V. Coates
Production Designer: John Box
Costumes: Phyllis Dalton
Art Director: John Stoll
Sound Recording: Paddy Cunningham
Sound Editor: Winston Ryder
Production Manager: John Palmer
Location Manager: Douglas Twiddy
Casting Director: Maude Spector
Set Dresser: Dario Simoni
Wardrobe: John Apperson
Property Master: Eddie Fowlie
Music: Maurice Jarre
Cast: Peter O'Toole (T. E. Lawrence), Alec Guinness (Prince Feisal), Anthony
Quinn (Auda abu Tayi), Jack Hawkins (General Lord Edmund Allenby), Jose
Ferrer (Turkish Bey), Anthony Quayle (Colonel Brighton), Claude Rains (Mr.
Dryden), Arthur Kennedy (Jackson Bentley), Donald Wolfit (General Sir
Archibald Murray), Omar Sharif (Sherif Ali)
Running Time: (1962) 222 minutes; (1971 reissue) 187 minutes; (1988) 218
minutes

Restoration Producers: Robert A. Harris and Jim Painten
Distribution: Columbia

1965
DOCTOR ZHIVAGO
Production Company: Carlo Ponti and David Lean
Executive Producer: Arvid L. Griffen
Producer: Carlo Ponti
Director: **David Lean**
Assistant Director: Roy Stevens and Pedro Vidal
Screenplay: Robert Bolt, based on the novel by Boris Pasternak
Photography: Freddie Young (35mm Panavision)
Production Designer: John Box
Art Director: Terence Marsh
Set Decorator: Dario Simoni
Special Effects: Eddie Fowlie
Costume Design: Phyllis Dalton
Editor: Norman Savage
Music: Maurice Jarre
Cast: Omar Sharif (Dr. Yuri Zhivago), Rod Steiger (Komarovsky), Julie
Christie (Lara), Tom Courtney (Pasha), Ralph Richardson (Alexander), Alec
Guinness (Gen. Yevgraf Zhivago), Geraldine Chaplin (Tonya)
Running Time: 193 minutes
Distribution: Metro-Goldwyn-Mayer

1970
RYAN'S DAUGHTER
Production Company: Faraway Productions; A.G. Film-MGM
Producer: Anthony Havelock-Allan
Associate Producer: Roy Stevens
Director: **David Lean**
Screenplay: Robert Bolt
Photography: F. A. Young (70mm Panavision)
Camera Operator: Ernest Day
Editor: Norman Savage
Production Designer: Stephen Grimes
Art Director: Roy Walker
Set Decorator: Josie MacAvin
Construction Manager: Peter Dukelow

Costumes: Jocelyn Rickards
Make-up: Charles Parker
Music: Maurice Jarre
Cast: Sarah Miles (Rosy Ryan), Robert Mitchum (Charles Shaughnessy), Trevor Howard (Father Collins), Christopher Jones (Randolph Doryan), John Mills (Michael), Leo McKern (Thomas Ryan), Barry Foster (Tim O'Leary)
Running Time: 206 minutes
Distribution: Metro-Goldwyn-Mayer

1979
LOST AND FOUND: THE STORY OF COOK'S ANCHOR
Production Company: Faraway Productions
Director: **David Lean**
Writer: Robert Bolt
Cinematography: Eddie Fowlie
Running Time: 40 minutes

1984
A PASSAGE TO INDIA
Production Company: Columbia Pictures
Producer: John Brabourne and Richard B. Goodwin
Associate Producer: John Heyman & Edward Sands
Director: **David Lean**
Screenplay: **David Lean**, based on the book by E. M. Forster
Music: Maurice Jarre
Cinematography: Ernest Day
Film Editing: **David Lean**
Production Design: John Box and Herbert Westbrook
Art Direction: Cliff Robinson, Leslie Tomkins, Herbert Westbrook, and Ram Yedekar
Costumes: Judy Moorcroft
Art Director: John Stoll
Cast: Judy Davis (Adela Quested), Victor Banerjee (Dr. Aziz H. Ahmed), Peggy Ashcroft (Mrs. Moore), James Fox (Richard Fielding), Alec Guinness (Professor Godbole), Nigel Havers (Ronny Heaslop), Richard Wilson (Turton), Antonia Pemberton (Mrs. Turton), Michael Culver (Major McBryde)
Running Time: 163 minutes
Distribution: Columbia

## *As Editor*

1930    *The Night Porter*
1931    *These Charming People*
1932    *Insult*
1933    *Money for Speed; Matinee Idol; The Ghost Camera; Tiger Bay; Song of the Plough*
1934    *Dangerous Ground; Secret of the Loch; Java Head*
1935    *Escape Me Never; Turn of the Tide*
1936    *Ball at the Savoy; As You Like It*
1937    *Dreaming Lips; The Last Adventures*
1938    *Pygmalion*
1939    *Spies in the Air; French Without Tears*
1940    *Spy for a Day*
1941    *Major Barbara; 49th Parallel*
1942    *One of Our Aircraft is Missing*

# DAVID LEAN

## INTERVIEWS

# David Lean on What You Can Learn from Movies

## CHARLES REYNOLDS/1958

D A V I D   L E A N is one of the top directors working in films today. His productions of *Brief Encounter, Great Expectations, Oliver Twist,* and *Breaking the Sound Barrier,* were all superior movies. Now Lean has completed one of the outstanding films of recent years, *The Bridge on the River Kwai.* David Lean, during an exclusive interview with *Popular Photography,* spoke of how the amateur movie maker can learn from professional films.

Q:   *Do you believe that the same principles are involved in making a good amateur film as a good professional film?*
A:   Absolutely the same. The only difference lies in the ambitiousness of the production, but a good film is good on any level, amateur or professional.

Q:   *Then you believe that the amateur can learn something about film technique from watching good professional movies?*
A:   Certainly, if he watches them in the proper way.

Q:   *How would you advise an amateur to watch a film in order to learn from it? For example, how would you advise the amateur to watch* Bridge on the River Kwai?
A:   I would hope that he would be quite incapable of appreciating the technique of the film. I think that really good film making conceals technique. If a film is really successful, the audience should be so caught up in it that they do not notice how it was made.

Q:   *Do you think then that to really study a movie you should see it more than once, the first time for impact and to enjoy it, and the second time to learn from it?*

---

From *Popular Photography* (no. 42, 1958). Reprinted by permission of Charles Reynolds.

A:    This sounds like a plug, but I think so. To really study a film you should have reached the point where you are no longer involved in the dramatic action. In a sense you must become bored with the story before you can study the technique. Of course as you become more and more accustomed to watching films in this manner you will automatically become more sensitive to technique on the first viewing.

Q:    *Did you use this technique in learning?*
A:    In my younger days I used to spend hours in movie houses to watch the cutting.

Q:    *From a technical standpoint what do you think is the mark of a good film?*
A:    It tells its story in pictures. This is always the problem of good film making. This is one of the biggest things that can be learned from any good movie. The amateur who wants to learn from viewing films should try to constantly notice how the director is telling his story in terms of visuals. "How can I show it?" is the question the director must constantly ask himself. Of course, it is faster in shooting and much easier to tell a story in dialogue, but it is never as effective. Dialogue compared to visuals is a bore; you are using a *moving picture* camera.

Q:    *Rene Clair has said that a deaf person watching a genuine film, may miss an important element of the film but need not miss the essence of it. Do you agree?*
A:    I think that's true. If you tell everything in words the members of the audience do not participate. The meaning is shoved at them. If you show them, they must put two and two together in order to get the meaning and are participating.

Q:    *In the last couple of years, with several devices for interlocking tape recorders or projectors on the market, it has become possible for the 8- and 16-mm movie maker to add sound to his films. What techniques can you suggest in the use of sound?*
A:    The best rule is "Never tell them what you can show them." Sound should give the film another dimension. It should be used as orchestration to give something the picture isn't giving. Anyone can take a shot of seagulls and put in their cries on the soundtrack but this doesn't really add anything. At the same time you can show a shot of gulls and by adding sound of waves with their cries you can suggest an entire beach scene. Sound can also be used to emphasize a point. In *Bridge* we used the screech of the bird to coincide with the cut to the young Japanese soldier who is being pursued through the jungle. This is the first time he is seen again since the beginning of the chase. The sound gives this important shot an added jolt to emphasize it.

Q:   *What other important principles can the amateur learn from watching films?*
A:   Of course there are many, but one of the most important is *selectivity*. Notice how the director uses his camera as a selective instrument to point up the
really significant part of the scene. When a painter works on a painting, he is
always selective, he only paints the things that are significant. The camera is
not naturally selective. This is the importance of a good cameraman. He must
work with the director to get the shot that emphasizes the most important part
and deemphasizes the rest. This is done through choosing the proper angle,
lighting, and also focus. When I was directing *Brief Encounter* we experimented
with an extreme technique of emphasis. In the closing scenes of the picture,
when Celia Johnson is sitting in the railroad station and listening to the train
that is taking her lover away for the last time, we took down the lights of the
room behind her and even faded out the voice of the woman talking to her, so
that all the emphasis was on her face and the sound of the departing train. This,
of course, is an extreme example but every shot in a film must face this problem
of selectivity. Now that many amateur-film makers have turrets on their 8- and
16-mm cameras, they are able to use different focal-length lenses to aid in this
selectivity. I learned a lot about this from watching American films. I used to
wonder why it was that American films seemed so much more "in" on their
characters than the continental films. Even if the image was the same size, the
American film seemed to have more impact. I found out that Hollywood used
longer focal-length lenses. There is always a temptation among inexperienced
film makers to be "greedy" and use a wide-angle lens to get everything. The
trouble is that it isn't concentrated. Instead of trying to get it all in one, it is
much better to make two shots out of it. Shot number one should say, "This is
the location." It should orient the audience. Then the following shots should
go in closer with a long-focus lens for the important details and "damn the
scenery." You can take two shots—one with a wide-angle lens and one with a
long lens. By having your camera closer to the subject with the wide lens you
can have the image the same size. Still, the shots with the long lens will have
more intimacy and impact because the depth of focus is less. The more concentration I want in a scene the longer lens I use. These lenses have a wonderful
quality about them which is better on the screen than through the viewfinder.

Q:   *What other techniques can one learn from studying the films he sees?*
A:   There are several common shortcomings in amateur films that can be
remedied and a lot can be learned about how to conquer them by observing
how directors in other films manage it.

First, amateurs rarely take enough footage to cover what they are trying to
show. If you are taking a long shot you must hold it on the screen long enough

to see what's in it. When I take a shot I try to do a little running commentary to myself on what the audience is supposed to see. "Isn't that a beautiful road, look at the tall trees, look at that dog crossing the road." That sort of thing. Each shot must be held long enough to tell its story and then make room for the next.

Second, never move your camera unless there is a reason for it. Notice in movies you view how all pans are motivated. Whenever you decide to pan, a little red warning light should go on in your mind and you should ask, "Can I do this better in a cut?" Amateur films often have too much panning.

Third, watch foregrounds. Photography is two dimensional and the picture must have planes to give it depth. Without these planes the shot will look like a "picture postcard." Often it is effective just to have a black object of some kind in the foreground. Don't light it. Keep it out of focus. In *Breaking the Sound Barrier* we needed a lot of aerial photography. It was all right but flat and uninteresting. So we had the special effects department put in an out of focus strut (by means of a traveling matte) across one corner of the frame. It added tremendously to the three-dimensional effect of the shot. In *Bridge*, we tried constantly to give depth by including foreground objects.

Finally, never take a shot that is not part of a whole. If you are going to take snapshots, don't use a movie camera. If you want a shot of some kids going down a hill on a toboggan, don't just take that shot and nothing else. That should be the climax of a sequence. Just using one shot is rushing that climax. Show the toboggan being taken out of the garage; show it moved to its position. Have closeups of the kids as they get on, show reactions of the onlookers. Any good movie that you will ever see is not built out of isolated shots but of sequences which build to climaxes.

# Out of the Wilderness

FILMS AND FILMING/1963

N o  t w o  p e o p l e  who knew Col. T. E. Lawrence agree completely as to his worth. Was he hero or knave, potential world conqueror or charlatan? Why did he weld together the warring tribes of the Arabian desert into a guerrilla army which broke the back of the Ottoman Empire during the years 1916–1918, and then, hailed as the "uncrowned King of Arabia," seek oblivion as an aircraftman in the Royal Air Force?

The new British film, *Lawrence of Arabia*, tries to answer those questions. It is produced by Sam Spiegel and directed by David Lean, who together made *The Bridge on the River Kwai*. In February 1960 Spiegel acquired the rights of Lawrence's autobiographical book *The Seven Pillars of Wisdom* from Prof. Arnold Lawrence who previously had refused to sell them to a film company. (A new edition of Lawrence's book has been published in Penguin Modern Classics.)

Much of the film has been photographed, in colour and wide screen, in Jordan, where many of Lawrence's exploits took place. The technicians found remnants of the Turkish railroad that Lawrence and his Arabs dynamited forty years ago—the metal laying unrusted in the sun. Some filming took place 250 miles east of Aqaba, near the Saudi Arabian frontier, a spot so desolate that not even the Bedouin go there.

Peter O'Toole, twenty-seven-year-old member of the Shakespeare Theatre Company, Stratford-on-Avon, was cast as Lawrence. Alec Guinness, who played Lawrence in Rattigan's *Ross*, plays the Emir Feisal. Jack Hawkins is cast as Sir Edmund Allenby and others in the cast include Anthony Quinn, Anthony Quayle, Claude Rains, and Jose Ferrer. Many of Lawrence's relatives, friends, and biographers have acted as technical advisers during the production.

---

From *Films and Filming* (no. 9, 1963). Reprinted by permission of the David Lean Estate.

DL:    One source for our film about T. E. Lawrence is his own book, *The Seven Pillars of Wisdom*; but we have read countless books about him. Robert Bolt has done the screenplay. We talked a lot about it; but it is virtually his own construction. It has nothing at all to do with the Terence Rattigan conception of Lawrence in his play, *Ross*. The script is essentially Bolt's conception of Lawrence. It is very close to my own conception of Lawrence, too. But for the people who actually knew Lawrence it may be unsatisfactory in a way that any screen biography would be unsatisfactory for someone who knew that particular person. An actor can never look like the person one knows so well, or speak as he did.

Consider the trouble one has in such a simple matter as taking a snapshot of a real person: it is difficult enough to please them with a photograph, let alone a film.

Q:    *Is your film an attempt to portray the whole of Lawrence's life?*
DL:    Except for a very short prologue we have dealt in the film only with Lawrence's two years in the desert. There is no RAF camp background. These two years were, in fact, Lawrence's whole life. Neither have we used any flashbacks to incidents in Lawrence's past life; although I hope his background is insinuated in the film.

In spite of the span of time being only two years we have an enormously long film. It will be at least three hours, perhaps nearer four.

We have had to use a lot of dramatic economy. Consequently we have short-circuited certain incidents, and run six characters into one. There were many military men concerned in the Lawrence story. It would be impossible to include them all in a screenplay so we have one (played by Anthony Quayle) who represents them as "an English military character," complementary to the role Jack Hawkins has as General Allenby. It is, I believe, the best performance Hawkins has ever given.

There were several political officers out there at the time and we have created one, a mixture suggested by various other characters, who we call Dryden, but who never really existed. Similarly, on the Arab side, we've used one young Arab character who is called Ali. He appears in *The Seven Pillars of Wisdom* quite a bit, but not in the way that we have used him. The most faithful Arab character we have is Sheik Auda (played by Anthony Quinn), a larger-than-life character, almost a bandit, a person Lawrence liked very much indeed. Sir Alec Guinness plays King Feisal, an authentic character.

People who know *Seven Pillars* well will say of the film "But it's not *Seven Pillars*," which indeed it isn't. That would take a film lasting twenty-four hours, so one has had to telescope and invent some incidents which may not have happened, in fact did not happen, but which we hope are nevertheless true for the overall picture of the man.

Q:   *How do you reflect his private life? Do you, for instance, accept that he was homosexual?*

DL:   In treating Lawrence as a character we have not been able to avoid, or indeed wanted to avoid, the controversial aspects of his private life. Our treatment for instance shows him to be masochistic. We have not implied that Lawrence was homosexual, though it depends on what you call homosexual. A lot of very early Hollywood epics, *Beau Geste* for instance, were homosexual; great manly friendships which, if psychoanalysed, might horrify the people who made the films and the people who acted in them. It is similar with Lawrence. I don't think he was a practising homosexual: and we haven't shown him as such.

Q:   *Does the script take sides politically?*

DL:   We have not avoided stating the facts of the political climate of the time, the British-Arab relationship; but the political arena was not our main concern.

Mostly I hope we have created a very exceptional hero. This is one of the things I am longing to find out when the film is seen by an audience. I don't know how an audience will take Lawrence as we have shown him: because in certain ways he is the full-blown traditional hero figure and he does some heroic things, but he also does things which will shock an audience. I think audiences are unaccustomed to this kind of shock. (And we are *not* making Lawrence another James Bond!)

Q:   *Has it been a difficult film to make?*

DL:   Peter O'Toole has the most difficult part as Lawrence. He's seldom off the screen. Other characters with new interest value pop up around him; but he has to carry the drama from start to finish. I believe his performance to be a very fine one indeed. By moving from location to location we had to shoot hopelessly out of continuity and this was difficult for both Peter and myself.

We were in Jordan for five months where we did all the big, spectacular desert material. Then we were in Spain where we did a lot of the interiors, not studio interiors but interiors of authentic Moorish buildings in and around Seville. It was better than working in Damascus because we were much nearer our home laboratory. Smaller exterior scenes were done among the dunes on the southern Spanish coast. Then we ended up in Morocco, south of the Atlas in a place called Ouarzazate. I shall never forget it; a terrible place. The production office was in a building that was once occupied by the French Foreign

Legion. During July and August when we were there they were sending the legionaires there as a punishment. The heat was tremendous.

The film has been shot on 65mm stock in the Panavision process. All the material we shot in Jordan we could not see until we returned to Britain. I sat in a projection theatre and saw it all in three sessions of three hours each, nine hours of material from that location alone. Fortunately with a cinematographer like Freddie Young I could be certain of the material I was getting.

Q:   *You started your career as a film editor. How does this affect your approach as a director?*

DL:   I supervise the editing myself, particularly the tricky action sequences. As I was an editor, it is hard to keep my hands off the celluloid. Nobody can prophesy at the script stage how a thing is going to be cut; but I try to shoot with a plan of the cutting in mind. I try to get the shots that I know will be wanted, moving the artists from here to there and not repeating the action all over again from another set-up. Sometimes one slips up and I curse myself for not having taken a long-shot which later I find was really necessary.

There is no one alive who at the shooting period can say exactly how it will be in the finished film. They can say how they think it will go; but ten per cent of their guesses will probably be wrong.

Robert Bolt has a wonderful visual sense, which helps the widescreen format; but he has also written some wonderful parts. If I were an actor who could play any of the parts, I would have great difficulty in choosing the one I wanted. The late Alex Korda once told me: "If you get a story with a good situation and two good characters you are half way home. If you get three good characters, you are very lucky. If you get four you can go down on your knees." And we have more than four.

It is remarkable that Bolt has scripted nothing before, although his plays *The Flowering Cherry* and *A Man for All Seasons* indicate the depth he can bring to character. It was our producer, Sam Spiegel's idea that he write the script. Although he has a great visual sense, I don't think there is a single scene that is there just for an "eyeful." For my part I would not have been happy filming the Lawrence story in black and white on a small screen ratio. Lawrence was bitten by the desert and by the people of the desert; and if you are going to show that, it must be in the best possible way, and there is nothing like this big screen process for showing it. It has its dangers. All sorts of people warned me at the beginning—"You can't be intimate on the big screen." I don't know if I have succeeded or not; I hope I have, because it is an intimate story really. The danger with a vast screen is that the audience is busy looking at something else and not the main characters.

I have concentrated on isolating characters by various means—lighting, the use of lenses.

Q:  *Has the casting been influenced by the need to find box-office names?*
DL:   In casting the film we have chosen the actors we thought most suitable for the parts. We were not primarily concerned with finding box-office names. It is obviously very useful for a producer to have names. If there was some un-known actor working at the Arts and we felt that Anthony Quinn was equally good, then we would go for Quinn naturally. The film has cost twelve million dollars (compared with the three million dollars spent on *The Bridge on the River Kwai*) and that approach to casting is a form of insurance.

Guinness played Lawrence on the stage; but for the film he is too old. The whole point about Lawrence is that he was twenty-eight years old at the time.

Q:  *Do you enjoy making expensive films like* The Bridge on the River Kwai *and* Lawrence of Arabia; *or would you be happier making smaller films with lower budgets?*
DL:   We have spent a lot of money. Yet I do not accept the popular idea that money is the great limiter; that a cheap film cannot be a good one. It depends on the subject. If one is going to do *Lawrence* properly one cannot do it cheaply. It costs a packet to take an enormous unit—cranes, lights, and thousands of extras—out into the desert. On the other hand it would be nutty to spend a lot of money on something like my early film, *Brief Encounter*. That was very cheap and I did it in ten weeks. I have been working on *Lawrence* for three years. If tomorrow I could find a subject I could do cheaply and in ten weeks, I would be absolutely delighted.

Perhaps I have become a "big film" man. What I think about the big film is this: I love travelling, going to strange corners of the world, and *Lawrence* gave me the opportunity of seeing places I could never possibly have seen in similar circumstances in private life. I was living in the desert and it was a wonderful experience. In order to travel this way you have to be physically very tough, and I haven't got so many more years to do that kind of thing. So if I can find the subjects, I would like to do another film in some strange place. Maybe it would not cost so much money, which would be better still because there wouldn't be such a circus going on around me.

Q:  *How do you rate one of your earlier, small budget films,* Brief Encounter?
DL:   I still have an affection for *Brief Encounter*. I have never really got over it. We were making *Great Expectations* when it came out, and I had the first print during our location work on Romney marshes. We got it down to the local cinema and screened it as a sneak preview. It started; and during the

first love scene a woman in the front row started laughing, a terrible cackling chicken's laugh. Then everyone else in the cinema started to laugh. And every love scene that came up, this woman started to laugh and the whole cinema was rolling in the aisles. I went back in the evening wondering how I could get into Denham Laboratories and burn the negative. I was so terribly ashamed of my work. So every time anyone mentions *Brief Encounter* I think "Oh yes, very nice in the art houses but what the hell happened out of town?" A lesson in humility may be good for everybody; but I didn't need a lesson in humility in those days, I was a very frightened young man.

I think the audience is generally right. A certain audience can be wrong about a certain type of picture; but generally, when an audience laughs in the wrong place, they're right. When there are things in a film that are a bit too near the bone, an audience will laugh for relief. I've had one or two of the *other* kind of laugh and I have thought "Yes, yes, quite right."

Q:    *Are partnerships a good thing or the industry—or not?*
DL:    In my early days I was working in partnership—Cineguild—with Ronald Neame and Anthony Havelock-Allan. Partnerships can be a very good thing, a part of growing up; you want to have close pals with you. After a bit, each member is bound to want to have a go themselves and so one branches out on one's own. This will happen to such contemporary partnerships as Bryan Forbes and Richard Attenborough; it is part of the logical creative process. It is how an art and an industry grows.

# The David Lean Recipe: A Whack in the Guts

## HOLLIS ALPERT / 1965

W H E N   T H E  great director game is played ("Who, in your opinion, is the greatest director in the world today?"), the parlor consensus will often nominate David Lean, a fifty-seven-year-old Englishman of Quaker parentage who has directed such outstandingly successful motion pictures as *Lawrence of Arabia*, *The Bridge on the River Kwai*, *Summertime*, *Great Expectations*, and *Brief Encounter*. Particularly in professional movie circles will Lean be the winner of the game, and those who choose him above men like Fellini of Italy, Kurosawa of Japan, and Bergman of Sweden, do so out of admiration for his mastery of film-making. Lean is, above all, a craftsman, an encyclopedia of technique and a subtle manipulator of audience emotions.

Lean himself admires the artistry and daring of Fellini's *8 1/2* and applauds the macabre brilliance of Stanley Kubrick's *Dr. Strangelove*, but he backs away from the notion that he, too, is an artist in film. "Film-making," he says simply, "is telling a story in pictures." But he will then go on to amplify that statement into a near infinitude of complexities, and it is not always easy to follow what he means. About the Kubrick picture, for instance, he said judiciously: "A truly professional job, but he took two degrees higher on the scale than I might have."

Lean represents something of a problem to movie critics and journalists. It is all but impossible to build up a *mystique* about him. He can't be discovered because he already ranks at the top. And he can't be toppled from his pedestal because his films are invariably made so well. He is, without a doubt, the world's most wanted director, though less honored in his own country than anywhere else.

In the United States, he has received two Academy Awards for directions (for *Lawrence* and *Kwai*). At home, most critics growl and grumble, faulting

From the *New York Times Magazine* (May 1965). Reprinted by permission of Hollis Alpert.

him for lack of humility, for using panoramic screen and color instead of the smaller screen and the black and white films a truer artist might employ. They complain that his more recent pictures are too big and too long and that he needs pots of money to make them. They admit he is gifted, but he doesn't play the game according to English rules.

He won't conform to any image, in fact. In spite of his large earnings, he owns no country home in Surrey and no town house in Chelsea. He does own a Rolls-Royce, but has had it fitted with left-hand drive because he is far more likely to use it on the Continent, than at home. But he really doesn't drive it that much anyway (though he admires the perfection of its manufacture). Between pictures he is more likely to lounge around his suite in the Grand Hotel in Venice or take a slow boat to India. "He might have been knighted long ago," one of his associates remarked, "if it hadn't been for that left-handed wheel on the Rolls." And he added: "David only lives, really lives, when he is making a picture."

Lean is very much alive at the moment, making a picture called *Doctor Zhivago* from the novel by Boris Pasternak. He is shooting it in Spain (mainly on the plain), with a side excursion to Finland, and is again using color and a panoramic screen. While he won't say exactly how much the film will cost, MGM, the distributor, is budgeting a minimum of $10 million and praying it won't go more than a million or two higher. Not that Lean is a waster of money—he is one of the fastest directors around when he needs to be—but he tries to get things on film that no one has attempted before. Or he asks others to get them—like the desert mirage in *Lawrence of Arabia*.

During the filming of *Zhivago* near Soria in northern Spain, the doctor (Omar Sharif) was saying good-by for the last time to his lifelong love, Lara, against a snow-covered landscape. Suddenly Lean said to his prop man: "Eddie, can you make it glisten?"

"I can," Eddie replied, "but it won't look real."

"I don't want it to," Lean said.

A few minutes later, cellophane had been spread over the snow-covered trees and bushes. "You see," Lean explained later, "I wanted it all to look not real, I wanted their *memory* of the scene all glistening in moonlight and with wolves howling in the distance." Although shot by daylight, the effect of moonlight would be achieved through special filters and color processing— and the wolves, of course, added to the sound track.

This time, Lean is not working with producer Sam Spiegel who, one may safely guess, would have liked him to direct his next superproduction, *The Chase* in which Marlon Brando will star. When Lean and Spiegel teamed for *Kwai* and *Lawrence*, a total of fourteen Oscars resulted and some $50 million was taken in by Columbia at the box-office. How many Oscars will Lean and Spiegel win separately? How many box-office dollars? Only time will tell how important each is to the other.

At present, Lean shows no sign of needing Spiegel, whose reputation as a producer is as good as Lean's as a director. It was Spiegel who made *Lawrence* possible for Lean by cornering the rights to make the film—a difficult job because of the many books written on Lawrence, including his own *The Seven Pillars of Wisdom*, and because other films about him had been planned for years. Spiegel has a sharp tasteful eye when it comes to evaluating a script; and above all, he is a master at deal-making and budget-watching. The cost of *Lawrence* would have been much higher if Lean had been allowed to have his way. Trade circles avow that Lean, who is entitled to a profit percentage of each film he now makes, eventually loses out on this end because of his time-consuming perfectionism, and once penalized financially is inclined to be cavalier about mounting costs.

Though it is not confirmed by either party, it is said that Lean was decidedly unhappy about being pulled—prematurely, he thought—out of the Jordanian desert by Spiegel after ten months there in 120 degree heat filming *Lawrence*. Spiegel thought that some scenes could be shot in Spain at savings in time and money. After a reputed hassle, Lean did go to Spain, fretting about the interruption to the shooting schedule.

Rumors were also current at the time that Lean had become "desert-happy" and had identified himself with the heroes of his epic. "Making a film does get to be a drug for me," Lean admits. "Once started it's hard for me to stop." But out of the fascination the desert had for him came some of the most haunting and unusual desert scenes ever captured on film. There were those in the audience who became desert-happy, too.

Lean is a handsome man, six feet tall, with a hawklike profile and heavy-browed eyes. His low blood pressure is said to account for the fact that he starts each workday slowly and then seems to wind himself up into a sustained intensity that often results in overtime for his crew. John Box, scenic designer for *Lawrence* and *Dr. Zhivago* and a close friend of Lean during and between films, said of him: "In some ways he is like an actor, a dynamo working up and up to a high pitch. Speak to him in the midst of his concentration, and you'll get what we call 'the stare.' It's a very intense stare, and some people can't cope with it." Those who can cope with Lean and his stare are likely to stay on from one picture to the next.

"He is ruthless, dedicated, and selfish," said Omar Sharif, who plays the title role in *Dr. Zhivago* and who was chosen by Lean for the role of Sheikh in *Lawrence*. "But he has not a trace of self-indulgence."

Sharif ascribes to Lean his rise to international stardom. "Everyone," he said, "has someone in his life who happens to him. David Lean happened to me." He has happened to others, too—Peter O'Toole, for example. Marlon Brando was originally thought of for the role of Lawrence and then Albert Finney. But when both hedged about committing themselves for a starting date, O'Toole was brought from Stratford, where he was playing Shylock, and asked to do a color test. Lean stopped the test in the middle. "No use shooting another foot of film," he said. "The boy is Lawrence."

Not that Lean is against working with established stars. He says, in fact, that "a director is paid in direct ratio to the number of stars who will work with him. It's a great advantage to have a star, if he's good." But when it came to casting of *Doctor Zhivago*, he vetoed most of MGM's suggestions, insisted upon Sharif, and chose others whose names do not automatically impress exhibitors. Julie Christie, a young British actress, got the plum part of Lara; Tom Courtenay got an important role, as did Rita Tushingham, and, chanciest of all, the youthful inexperienced Geraldine Chaplin was picked to play Zhivago's patient wife. (Whatever risks are involved will no doubt be offset by the presence of such big names as Sir Alec Guinness, Sir Ralph Richardson, and Siobhan McKenna.)

"Geraldine came to see me," Lean said, "wearing jeans, her hair all screwed up at the back and looking about sixteen. But I gave her a test with a result that was touching and wonderful." He tartly dismissed the suggestions that he was using Miss Chaplin because of her father's name. He is in a hunch-playing mood for *Dr. Zhivago* and Geraldine is one of his hunches. "I wanted actors who could look twenty," he said, "and they don't exist. The established people are all middle-aged ladies and gentlemen, so I decided to take the plunge on youth and make stars of my own."

He read *Dr. Zhivago* for the first time while sailing to New York to talk over the possible film projects for the future. The book had been sent to him by Carlo Ponti, who had obtained the film rights from the Italian publisher. Before his boat docked, Lean had decided to do it, and thus Ponti became the producer.

The film is only Lean's third in ten years. When he is not working, if he has any home at all, it is his hotel suite in Venice. He loves Venice, and when there does little, he admits, except "get up late and lounge around. I become frightfully lazy after a picture." His fourth wife, Leila, regarded as one of India's most beautiful women, ruefully describes herself as all but divorced when her husband is working on a film, which includes developing the script with the screenwriter. After seeing a picture through its final editing phase and its premiere, he will join her, usually in Venice.

When he finished *Lawrence*, he went off with her on a slow boat to India, where he went on picture-taking expeditions throughout the country. "He loves cameras," said John Box. "They fascinate him because they're so perfectly made. He admires the precision of fine machinery." Box and Lean once took a trip to Scandinavia, where each clicked away with cameras in friendly competition. One day Lean handed Box an expensive Hasselblad. "It's not a gift" he said, "but simply so we can start off even."

Lean takes great pride in his still pictures. Box once asked him why he troubled himself to photograph a drearily uninteresting prospect. "Because it's cold and horrible and miserable," he said.

"The true key to David Lean," Box theorized, "is his professionalism. This confounds his intellectual English critics. They want him to be an intellectual. But he isn't one, nor does he pretend to be one. He is, and wants to be, a professional."

Queried on the subject, Lean explained what professionalism meant to him. "It's the application of the practical to the gift. It's shutting up and doing it. The English love the amateurs and are highly suspicious of the pros—that old thing of gentlemen versus players. The sports pages of the English newspapers show this patronizing attitude towards those who practice their sport professionally. It's of course quite different in America." Nothing quite excites his admiration so much as a revelation of professionalism in action.

He remembered directing Katharine Hepburn in a scene for *Summertime*. "I had to get her to a window to look out at something," he said. "No earthly reason for it, and I told Kate that I just wanted her to look out the window.

"'Don't apologize,' Miss Hepburn said. 'That's my job—to make it look natural.'

"And she did," Lean said. "Did it splendidly. An amateur actress couldn't have done that, would have needed motivation and all that sort of thing."

Having done it, Katharine Hepburn landed on Lean's list of professionals. "Omar Sharif is a born pro," he said, enthusiastically, meaning perhaps that he was ruthless, dedicated, and selfish, but not in the least self-indulgent. "He gives all he's got." But, having worked with Sir Alec Guinness on *Great Expectations*, *Oliver Twist*, *Kwai*, and *Lawrence*, and though Guinness got an Academy Award for his portrayal of the stiff-necked British colonel in *Kwai*, Lean was not yet ready to admit Sir Alec into his inner circle of professionals.

This is because Guinness generally has his own fairly fixed ideas about the roles he plays, and for all his politeness can be a stubborn sort of chap. "It was like a game of tennis with him in *Kwai*," Lean said. "I'd throw him a ball and he'd throw me one. In the end I forced him. We had stand-up rows. It was necessary and I had to do it." Ironically, Guinness is again working with Lean in *Dr. Zhivago*, temperamental differences notwithstanding.

Lean, who is meticulous when it comes to the mechanics of picture-making, is thus equally exacting with his actors. Each is a separate problem to be solved.

"In the first two weeks," he said, "you can get a pretty good smell about what each one needs. They're all of them frightened rabbits basically. And, let's admit it, it's a frightening job for them. It's *their* mug up there on the screen. Most of the time, directing actors is a matter of gentle suppression and gentle encouragement. If they're inclined to be brash, I suggest soft, sensitive things for them to do."

When working with Peter O'Toole, however, his direction came close to collaboration. "Some of us felt he had identified, personally with Lawrence," one of his technicians said. Lean saw to it that O'Toole rode a camel like an Arab, cultivating in him a mixture of intensity and flamboyance.

Sharif who had developed a florid style of acting when making a couple of dozen Middle Eastern epics in Cairo and elsewhere, encountered a Lean he described as "cold-blooded." Lean kept a stopwatch on him as he rehearsed and played his scenes.

"I once asked David," Sharif said, "what he thought was the most difficult thing for a director to know.

"Lean answered without hesitation: 'How fast an actor should speak.'"

That was the reason for his use of the stopwatch, held either by himself or his script supervisor. "I'll tell the actor to do the scene three times," Lean said. "The first time in forty seconds, the second in thirty-seven, the third in thirty-five. When he thinks he's done it as rapidly as possible, I'll tell him, 'now we'll shoot it in thirty.' The actor always thinks he is rushing it, but as a rule the fastest take is the best. Following this process through a whole film builds simplicity and economy. You can't afford frills in a film."

For all his remarkable track record as a director, which began with his co-directing of Noel Coward's *In Which We Serve*, Lean thinks of movie-making as a series of compromises. For him there is never enough time, never enough money, and never the perfect actor for the role. "An actor," he said, "can't possibly be 100 per cent right for a part. There's your first compromise. And, as for the technical part, a line must be drawn somewhere. You must stop eventually. At what point do you call the halt? That's the line of compromise."

Lean still has his regrets about *Lawrence*. "We had only the first part of the script finished when I began shooting," he said. "I'll never do that again, because it necessitated an interruption midway, and there was an imbalance between the two parts." After the film opened, he took it and lopped twenty minutes from its three and three quarter hours. "So many critics talked about its excessive running time, and this began to bother the exhibitors. I did the cutting myself. I'm quite objective about it now. On the other hand, I don't want to have to do the same thing with *Dr. Zhivago*. Accordingly, he has pared the script, with playwright Robert Bolt, to a three-hour long bone.

"We work together very closely," he said about Bolt, who also did the script for *Lawrence*. "I won't call myself a writer. I do call myself a bit of a constructor, and a fairly good embroiderer. We first spent ten weeks hammering out a fifty-page line through the book, and that has become the shape of the film. We provide dramatic constructions where the book is not dramatic. A 283-page script emerged, which might have meant nearly four hours on the screen.

"We have this enormous subject, involving revolution and war, and a chronicle that starts with a small boy and continues until after his death. If cut down too much, it might seem just another love story. We tore our hair out trying to get economy, to cut out all the fat. And now it's down to the point where we can give an answer for every damn scene in the picture."

The director who is so totally absorbed in movie-making was not allowed to attend movies during his boyhood in Croydon, near London, where he was born March 25, 1908. His Quaker family regarded them as sinful, and David could only listen enviously while his pals talked of the moves they had seen. His father, an accountant, sent him to a Quaker school in Reading called Leighton Park. There he was free to go to the movies, and fell in love with them.

"By the time I was nineteen," Lean said, "I was spending all my spare time at the movies, and was mad about photography. An aunt suggested to my mother that I ought to try film work." He got himself a job at the Gaumot Studios just as the sound era was beginning, working his first month on a trial basis without salary. He was allowed to be the "tea boy," which meant that he brought tea in midmorning and midafternoon to the workers on the set, and rose quickly to be the number-board boy. (The number board, used at the beginning of each shot, identifies the move being made and each individual take.)

After running messages for a while, he reached the status of third assistant director, which "mainly meant fetching players to the set." The cutting rooms intrigued him most of all, however, and he devoted himself to learning film editing thoroughly. He soon developed an eye for the most effective shots, and found he had a gift for developing them into an understandable continuity. Even now, for him, "the fun begins with editing."

His rise as an editor was spectacular, and by the mid-thirties he was known as "the highest paid cutter in pictures." Among his triumphs as a film editor were *Pygmalion*, with Leslie Howard, and *Major Barbara*, with Rex Harrison and Wendy Hiller (who was also in "Pygmalion"). It is through editing and the canny use of the sound track that he often achieves his most striking effects. In the opening scenes of *Kwai*, as the British prisoners march into their

Japanese prisoner-of-war compound, glimpses of their all but shoeless feet are contrasted with their proud military bearing and the stirring whistling of the Colonel Bogie march.

"It sometimes takes nerve," he said, "to get an effect you visualize. I've found it necessary to reduce an audience to near-boredom in order to give it a whack in the guts."

He cited the scene in which Omar Sharif first appears out of a desert mirage and seems to be approaching in slow motion a water hole at which Lawrence has stopped with an Arab guide. The scene explodes with electrifying shock when Sharif shoots the Arab dead for using the water hole without permission—in the midst of a desert of magnificent endless solitude. "What made the scene," Lean said, "was the near-boredom of the three minutes of preparation."

None of the critics mentioned the scene, however. "Ninety per cent of the critics," he said, "fall over in helpless admiration at the directorial stuff that isn't difficult to do—the show–off stuff. I'm bothered by this sort of worship only because the stuff is so very easy to do. It's always been important to me to hide the technique. Even when doing the most touching scene, as in *Brief Encounter*—I actually cried while doing some of that picture—in the back of my mind was a desire to knock spots off the audience. Really, half this business is putting a rectangle around things. Put a square around something someone is looking at and he'll say surprise, 'Oh, how beautiful.' And don't think it's the photographer who provides the square. I do."

Lean's present eminence was not reached without occasional reverses. After Noel Coward had averred publicly that he owed a great deal of the excellence of *In Which We Serve* to Lean's direction of the action sequences, he granted a choice of his plays to Lean and to Ronald Neame, Lean's cameraman, for production as films. Lean and Neame chose *This Happy Breed*, then went on to *Blithe Spirit* and *Brief Encounter*. The tamer British critics were not happy about either of the latter, although they were commercially successful.

Lean and Neame then turned to Dickens, making *Great Expectations* and *Oliver Twist*. Alec Guinness's playing of Fagin was alleged to have overtones of anti-Semitism, and when the film was finally released in the United States, after being held up for three years, American audiences saw only a severely edited version.

It was at this point that he encountered setbacks which, for a time, threatened his career. In 1949, he divorced his second wife, British actress Kay Walsh, and married actress Ann Todd. With Miss Todd he made the two worst pictures of his entire career *Madeleine* and *One Woman's Story*, and some have linked their failure, artistically and commercially, to excessive loyalty to and fascination with his wife. *Madeleine* was an almost endless series of beautiful close-ups of the enigmatic face of Miss Todd, who played a woman accused of murder. The end of the film left her guilt in doubt.

As for *One Woman's Story*, it was regarded as soap opera of the kind Hollywood did with more éclat. (Oddly enough, some British intellectual critics have recently come around to regarding these two films as the best of his work, holding *Kwai* and *Lawrence* to be relatively inferior.) After the double debacle with Ann Todd, Lean came back to make the critically acclaimed *The Sound Barrier*, in which she had a lesser and more appropriate role.

Lean tends to stay aloof from esthetic evaluation of his films. Putting frames around pictures is what he essentially regards as his craft. But he would prefer not to have to do this in a studio. "I'm bored with studio pictures," he said. "I cannot bear going on sound stages. I love the medium, but it can't really move in drawing rooms."

And it is for this reason that he has taken on the large scale subjects of the last ten years. He would have made *Dr. Zhivago* in the Soviet Union if the Russians had let him. "They invited me to come and talk to them, but I knew it was to talk me out of making the picture."

As for the picture's message, Lean thinks it will be very close to the theme of the book. "Pasternak said, in effect, that here is a great big human earthquake; this lot of people thinks it worth it, this other lot says maybe. And it seems to me Pasternak says it is not worth it in terms of human suffering, but doesn't underline it. We do the same thing."

With this film, as with his others, he speaks of himself mainly as an interpreter. "I'm not a first-class artist," he said. "I've come up through the ranks of the technicians. I'm really Mr. Middlebrow. If I had something to say, really to say, I would write a poem or a book. But I'm putting into pictures something that's already there, something that's already said, and attempting to make it visual."

Some wonder if this modesty, though becoming, is sincere. Note the size and scope, the largeness of the effort involved in these last three films.

"It takes terrific energy to do a big picture," he says in answer to this. "I want to do them while I can, and I don't have many more years."

No one has noticed any slackening of his energy during the making of *Dr. Zhivago*. And John Box, for one, thinks he will be attracted to another large subject after finishing it. "David," he said, "whether he is aware of it or not, has a passion for getting to know the world he lives in, and he'll continue to explore it, either with a Hasselblad or a 70-mm film camera."

# David Lean Interview

ROBERT STEWART / 1 9 6 5

RSS: *The first thing I would like you to talk about if you would is how you begin making a movie? Do you pick a book, do you visualize something photographically, what is the process, how do you begin? Using* Zhivago *as an example, or any of the movies you've made, what is the inception for a director?*

DL:   As far as I'm concerned, it's, as it were, a kind of falling in love. I love making movies. If I wasn't paid to do it, I would pay to do it. And I look around for something that is going to fascinate me. And it may come in various ways. I have heaps of books sent in to me. A terrible flood happens at the end of a picture, if it's a good one, and producers and agents whip up all sorts of books. About 99 percent, as far as I'm concerned, don't click with me. On the other hand one might, as, in fact, was the case with *Zhivago*. I might get an idea of my own. A long time ago I made a film called *Breaking through the Sound Barrier*, which came as the result of me reading an article in the evening paper about Geoffrey de Havilland, whose plane had crashed, and it said that perhaps he had exceeded the speed of sound and this could possibly break up an aeroplane. That gave me the idea for that film. And then sometimes I've seen a play on the stage which I've liked. I don't know, it can happen so many ways.

RSS: *What is the feeling when you fall in love with a project. What goes on after you've read a book like* Zhivago? *Do you begin to imagine scenes, do you begin by thinking of the characters, or do you begin by thinking of the dramatic action or something that stirs you? What begins the process?*

DL:   I think it's almost entirely emotional. For instance, when I read *Zhivago*, my common sense told me that it was a terribly difficult thing to undertake, but I was so fascinated by the book, I was so moved by it. I think that was one

---

Portions of this interview were published in the *Atlantic Monthly* under the title, "*Dr. Zhivago*: The Making of the Movie." Full interview reprinted by permission of Robert Stewart.

of the great things about it. I've done two films now with no women in them, and I like love stories very much and I found this a superb love story. I just thought, "This must make a marvelous movie. God knows how I'm going to do it. But if we're clever enough, it will come out." And as a matter of fact the one stipulation I made was that I'd do it if Robert Bolt wrote the script. I have done quite a bit of scriptwriting myself, but this was completely beyond me, far too difficult. And it required somebody with a certain classical background, a real expert. And I think Robert is that.

RSS: *How do you view the relationship of the director to the screenplay? I would imagine that you see them as very closely related and very closely allied in producing a movie, in terms of getting the characters translated from prose into dialogue, in terms of putting the dramatic action into some workable form.*

DL: I think that the script of course is the most important thing in the whole film. If you haven't got a good script, you cannot make a good film. You can mess up a good script and make a bad film, but I don't think that you can make a good film out of a bad script. And when I first worked with Robert on *Lawrence of Arabia*, I said to him that the person that I most wanted to please was he, the writer. He didn't believe me. I think he does now. I have enormous respect for the writer. He's the man who gives the actors their words. He gives them their characters. He gives them really everything. And he also gives me what I have to interpret from the visual point of view.

RSS: *Assuming that you have received a screenplay that meets your requirements, how do you make that interpretation? What do you do then when you get a screenplay?*

DL: Well, it doesn't quite work like that. I've never gotten a screenplay and gone to work on it. I've always worked on it. In some cases I've contributed a lot to the writing. In others I've contributed little. In the case of Robert Bolt, I have been with him all the time and we discuss every scene. He has a go at writing a scene. We discuss it. And he may rewrite it, and in fact some scenes have been rewritten many times, and by the time it comes for me to shoot the film I know what both of us are after.

In fact, it goes so far that with Robert—it's the first time I've ever done it—I get him to read the whole script to a tape recorder. And whenever I want to refer to anything, I play this tape when I'm doing a scene and I'm not sure the way he intended a certain line, and he makes comments. We've discussed the scenes backwards and forwards, we've agreed how they go, and it's a wonderful reminder to me. It's surprising what one forgets; when one wrote a scene, say six months ago, at the time you think, "Oh I'll never forget that." But you do. And I find that this tape recording business works very well.

RSS:    *What do you mean when you say you're after something visual? This I would imagine, at least to the average moviegoer, is always what the director stands for, the visual, the taking of the script and putting it into the audience's eye. How do you imagine Zhivago walking through the snow or do you have a feeling about his actions? How do you see the picture coming out from the screenplay or after you've read the book or when you get behind the camera?*

DL:    It's a terribly difficult question but I'll try to explain. Do I imagine it? I think I do, yes. It's rather a dreamlike imagination. And I could tell you that I imagined Zhivago walking into a room and sitting down on a chair. And if you asked me, "Where's the window?" I'd say, "Oh my goodness, I hadn't thought of there being a window, of course, there must be windows." Unless the window was, of course, an essential part of the action with him. So that's why I call it dreamlike, because there are certain parts of it that are absolutely blank. But I have, how shall I say it, a kind of smell of what a scene should be like. Let me put it another way: it's as if I've got a negative—talking negatives and positives in a photographic sense—I've got an imaginary negative in my mind, and when I get on the set, I try to make a positive which will match that negative. And I will find myself very often saying to an actor, "No, not that, do it softer." If he said to me, "Why?" I wouldn't be able to tell him; I just know it wasn't as I felt it should be in my original feelings about the scene. It's a kind of mood thing, I suppose. I don't know if that makes any sense at all.

RSS:    *It makes good sense. When you have the positive of this negative do you then know?*

DL:    That's right. And other times something will happen and I won't say a word, and we'll shoot right away and that's it. Because I just haven't got anything to say, because it works well. It seems to fit in with my imagination of the thing. And, of course, we've discussed these scenes like mad. We know exactly what we're after in a scene. Whether I get it or not is another question, but we do know what we're after. And I'm really, I suppose, trying to please Robert. And better him as a matter of fact. I have a sort of game, if I can beat the script.

You ask me about visuals, I mean, long shot, Zhivago leaves the front door of the house, runs across the street, and jumps onto a tram, cut, interior of a tram. Now if I can make that long shot of him running across the street better than Robert and I visualized in the first place, by having a little bit of something extra, something in the composition perhaps or another bit of action in the street, I'm absolutely delighted. And I have a sort of game like that. I think I call it beating the script. And if I beat the script, I'm very lucky. Most of the time I'm quite behind our dreams of scenes.

RSS:    *What are some of the particular problems in* Zhivago? *I suppose the scope of Russia, for example, might be one problem, or the revolution, or the contrast between the personalized love story and the revolution. What are some of the problems or the major negatives which have to be put into positives?*

DL:    I think one of the most difficult things in *Zhivago* is the character of Zhivago, himself, because he's not a typical screen hero. He is an observer. He doesn't do anything really. Events happen around him and this doesn't often happen on the screen. The hero is always the doer. A very, very difficult part, I must say, because one's got to resist the temptation to make him heroic in the ordinary sense. And, of course, the risk is that one makes him dull. And so one's got to keep one's nerve and say, "That's not it, don't glamorize it, don't glamorize it, play it down, play it straight." You know that sort of thing.

And the other great difficulty is really on the same lines, that it's a love story about a very, very good man who has two women in his life and he loves both of them. Now this obviously can happen in real life, but in the movies it doesn't. Generally, a man's got a good wife and is in love with a bitch whom he can't resist, or something like that. Or he's got a bitchy wife and is in love with the good girl around the corner. This isn't the case. They're both marvelous women, and I don't know how film audiences will take it. I don't think they've seen it.

RSS:    *How do you feel about Russia and the revolution and the setting of this? Do you think this inspires the love story or gives it a frame of reference in the way the desert seemed to almost in a way be the frame of reference in* Lawrence of Arabia?

DL:    Yes, in a way. It happens to be the Russian revolution, but it's really about a great, big human earthquake. It might be the Russian revolution or some other revolution or something quite different. But I wouldn't say it's political, you know. Not a good answer, I can't answer that.

RSS:    *It goes beyond politics I suppose.*

DL:    It isn't really political at all.

RSS:    *One wonders why the Russians ever banned the book in the first place. It just seems so human and not political at all, really.*

DL:    I can only imagine by having seen some Russian films that in the Russian movies the revolution is always glorious and in *Zhivago* it isn't always glorious. There are some dreadful things done and some dreadful people come up, as I think they must do in all revolutions. And I suppose this is just against the propaganda line. I don't know.

RSS:    *It reads very much like the descriptive novels of the French revolution, all the factions and the splitting off and the changing sides and the coming to power of so many different groups within such a short period of time. It really wasn't one way, as the Russians tried to give you that impression. What do you feel about the Russian setting? Do you like working with that sort of primitive medieval type? With Law-rence of Arabia, you seem to feel very comfortable with desert and the sun. It seemed to bring the picture to light. Do you feel that snow and the baroque Russian setting is helpful?*

DL:    It's very helpful. I hope I'm doing it right, actually. I hope it's wild enough, primitive enough. It's one of the reasons I'm very glad Omar Sharif is playing Zhivago, because he'll give a certain foreignness to it. I think the film would be a failure if it were a story of a lot of polite English ladies and gentle-men in Russian clothing, and I think Omar has a certain oriental something which, of course, he is, which should be in *Zhivago*.

RSS:    *How would you compare the character of Zhivago with that of Lawrence? Did you find any similarities? I think that they are the opposite in some ways. Lawrence, as you said, is doing things.*

DL:    Well, it's more than that. Lawrence was certainly doing things, but Lawrence, I think, also had a very great opinion of himself, feelings, which he himself said he despised terribly. Now, Zhivago has no opinion of him-self whatever; I think if somebody told him that he was a remarkable man, he would be astounded.

RSS:    *When Lara tells him how remarkable he is, he sort of faints, he can't bear it. He is so used to doing things and going. There is one point in the book when he comes back and finds that she's taken care of him. I think he actually falls unconscious, because it's such a shock to have things reversed and have someone loving him and taking care of him. And, I suppose, Lawrence is just the opposite, he always was.*

DL:    Well Lawrence was a doer, wasn't he, and great vanity too. And Zhivago has no vanity whatever.

RSS:    *Talking about* Lawrence of Arabia *and* Zhivago *and* The Bridge on the River Kwai, *about large movies, I think until that point* Brief Encounter *was the movie you were known by and that was such a small focused love story. Do you find it more comfortable to work with the larger?*

DL:    It isn't that really. Everybody asks me why make large movies. I suppose I enjoy doing it. I love traveling. For *Bridge on the River Kwai*, I went to Ceylon, spent a year there which was very fascinating. On *Lawrence* I spent the same time in the desert, living in a caravan, seeing things that very, very, very few people are privileged to see. On this for instance I've just come back from Fin-land, seeing a completely different part of the world, and we're doing most of the movie in Spain, which I like very much.

Now when you compare that with working down the mine in London somewhere, I don't think you'd be surprised why I choose these large movies. The idea of doing a completely studio picture now is horrible to me. I don't mind doing certain scenes in the studio, but it's a thing I'd rather like to do in about ten years' time if I'm still at it.

RSS:     *When you say you like traveling, do you like movies that have certain geography or is it just that you like the traveling and you—*
DL:     I like strange places, I must say, I like strange places.

RSS:     *Do you like them for a movie or do you—?*
DL:     Both. When I was young, I used to go to the movies a lot and movies used to show me a world that I thought I would never be able to see. And I think this went out of the window when the talkies came. They moved into drawing rooms, as it were, and the films were interesting enough, some of them, but I lost a lot of my keenness for the cinema. Now I've gone off the track. What I'm really trying to say is that the wonderful thing about the movie medium is that it can show people various parts of the world, customs, that they'd never see, that they can't see in any other medium.

RSS:     *Talking about talkies and silent films, how do you feel about movies today, in general, American movies versus Italian movies, or the new school of English movies? Are you interested in the change, do you think?*
DL:     The terrible thing is—and I have to be truthful and say I don't go to the cinema very often now—I find a lot of these new films very obtuse and obscure. I find them lacking in dramatic shape. And they seem more like diaries to me than drama. Many of them are greatly praised by the critics and I think that the critics have gone overboard a little bit. I think that if some of these films are seen in ten years' time—God knows what most films will look like in ten years' time—people will wonder why they were praised so lavishly. I like personally, old fashioned nowadays I suppose, I like a good strong story and I like a good strong dramatic construction.

RSS:     *When you talk about the diaries and the movies that lack dramatic action are you talking about the Fellini type movies and the Tony Richardson type movies?*
DL:     No, I think Fellini is simply terrific. He can do anything as far as I'm concerned, with a visual eye like he's got—I just sit back in admiration.

RSS:     *If I may interject, actually, the essential difference, in connection in with your interest, what you've been saying and writing, may be in cutting. The average moviegoer thinks the director walks down onto the set and has the script in front of him, and, indeed, some directors I'm sure do this, and just tell the actors what to do. Then when the picture's finished the cutter takes it to the cutting room and that's the end of it. But such is not the case. I've heard you say that the cutting is the thing you enjoy so much, putting it all together.*

DL:     Cutting, I must tell you, interests me almost more than directing.

RSS:     *What is a day or a week like in making* Dr. Zhivago, *for example? What is the process? First you go out and set up the set and then you look through the camera. If you could tell me how that goes about right through to the editing, that might help. But begin earlier than that, if I may suggest. When you got the book and you started to work with Robert Bolt on developing the script, you talked for months, weeks before putting anything on paper. Then you got a story outline. Talk about that just a little.*

DL:     What we did, we met early in January, actually, and we talked for quite a long time, and then we spent about a couple of months, ten weeks, doing an outline of the screenplay. Now it was, more or less, what we've got, more or less but at least it was a way through the wood. We changed certain things, but at least we had a beginning, a middle, and an end. We knew what characters were going to be in, what scenes were going to be in, what was going to be cut, which was more difficult still, and the points we were trying to make en route. Then Robert started writing, and he wrote a complete script with dialogue. And then we started again on the beginning of that and went through that with revision after revision after revision until we were, both of us, I think, pleased. And in the end, as far as the script was concerned, we were as pleased as we could be, with certain regrets, mostly cuts, because of the size of the book, but we'd gotten what we imagined was the best we could do with it. That took about a year; we finished, I think it was November. We started in January and finished in November.

At the same time, of course, we were thinking about cast. This was a headache because there are some marvelous parts in this film, but they're not cliché movie parts: Zhivago himself and the two women, two girls, and what's more they have to be young. Now obviously when you're making a movie like this, which is very expensive, you want some star names, and this was a great headache because all the star names are not so young.

And at the same time John Box, the art director, and myself were trying to find where to shoot the picture, because this is Russia. We first of all went to Yugoslavia, had a wonderful time. I drove myself actually, had a 10,000-mile car trip from Rome to Yugoslavia, quite a trip there, then drove right up through Germany to Denmark, Stockholm, went all the way up to Sweden, over the Arctic circle and all the way down Finland. And then we finally came here to Spain.

And we decided to make the bulk of the picture in Spain for several reasons, one of them being that in these northern countries you cannot get big crowds, and *Zhivago* has some big crowd scenes, must have for this revolutionary stuff. And in Spain there are big crowds. And Spain also has a fantastic variety of scenery. For instance, the places we had found for some of the scenes which were supposed to be the Russian Steppes are much better than anything we saw in Finland or Sweden. Then, of course, there is the matter of expense; these northern countries are terribly expensive to work in. I suppose Finland is as expensive as America or France. We went up to Finland to do the snow scenes.

Then one's got to decide on the sets—the sets are terribly important, what the settings are going to be like, if one's going to make it a little larger than life, if one's going to make it dead realistic, what style, in other words, one's going to adopt. And this is quite a job, quite a matter for experiment.

The costumes require a tremendous lot of research, because we've got to recreate Russia, and the costumes are quite a job in themselves. We got books and books and reproductions of photographs and illustrations, and I think we've done, or at least the art department, have done very well on this. I think that they do look Russian.

After the script is finished, after Robert Bolt has done his job, I myself do what's called a shooting script. I type it all out on two fingers, the whole script, and I sit down and I try to imagine how I would like to see it appear on the screen, when to cut to close ups, when to have long shots, if it's a low angle, if it's a high angle, and so forth and so on. And I sit there and I try and translate it into pictures, very definite pictures, and this takes quite a time. I've forgotten how many scenes there are in the script, but, how many are there? Look at the last number there.

RSS:   *1,739.*

DL:   That's 1,739 shots, you see.

RSS:   *Robert Bolt doesn't do any of the . . . ?*

DL:   He didn't do that.

RSS:   *He does some of it.*

DL:   I wouldn't say that. Robert does, he does a lot. He does when it strikes him for a certain dramatic effect. But in Bolt's script whole pages go by without a change of shot, maybe. Other times he'll have about eight changes of shot on a page if he sees it that way. But I've got to go through. And what I do is prepare, as it were, a blueprint that will work. It works alright the way I do it.

Then I go on the set having this behind me, and I feel at perfect liberty to alter it. I don't mean the dialogue or the intention of the scene, but the way

I shoot it. In action scenes—when I say action scenes, I mean, for instance, we have in this, dragoons charging a crowd—I follow the script very closely; I copy the shots as I've written them in the script. In a dialogue scene, I won't take much notice of it. I'll get the actors there on the set, and we'll rehearse the scene and when the scene seems to me pretty good, I then try to think of how to photograph it. And if the scene is well rehearsed and it's a good scene and it's played well, the curious thing is that it falls automatically into camera angles. If I can't photograph a scene, I very often suspect that there is something wrong with the rehearsing or even something wrong with the writing. If the scene is well conceived, it acts well and it photographs well. It's one of those little mysteries I don't quite understand but it is the case.

RSS:   *After the scene is shot do you then look and see what you've got and then edit and put together or do them over?*

DL:   No, there's not much chance of doing anything over because of the frightening cost of making a movie. We're running at $27,000 a day. I daren't think of it. If I had a terrible fruit machine clicking that money out every minute of the day, I'd be paralyzed with fear, and we wouldn't be able to work and I daren't think of it. I can't. I've just got to do my best. You've got to be right first time and very often, of course, you're wrong first time. When finally you see the film cut together, you wish you'd done this and this and that and you're stuck with it.

And of course I never see the film, I can't see the film until I've finished it. Unlike a stage director who can run his play in a dress rehearsal, or any rehearsal for that matter, from start to finish and see the general shape of it. I'm more or less guessing and trying to match this negative that I've talked about, all the time. I don't even shoot in continuity. In this film, for instance, which covers a great period of time, I've had to do all the winter scenes first. Now those winter scenes are dotted about the script because there are many summers and winters. And I just have to back my judgment as to the dramatic peak reached with scenes that I haven't shot, when I have to insert something I've got to shoot right now.

RSS:   *That was going to be my last question, how you, as opposed to an actor or stage director, keep the line of a picture which may have several climaxes or one climax and several subclimaxes? How can you do that when you don't shoot in sequence?*

DL:   That's partly why I work—I saw you smile when I said I typed the whole script out on two fingers. It's a very, very good thing to do because typing it out on two fingers you get to know it very well indeed. And so before I've shot a foot of film, I have got very clear but vague, dreamlike impressions of the whole film, and I just have to rely on that. Sometimes, of course, I'm wrong, and I kick myself and wish I'd started a certain scene on a higher emotional key, because I hadn't realized that the scene before was going to work and build up to such a height. And it's a great matter of luck really. I don't know, it's a funny job.

RSS: *You wouldn't do anything else.*
DL: No, that I wouldn't, no.

RSS: *Did you ever think of the stage as opposed to movies, where the line of a part would be more direct from one end to the other?*
DL: Not really, it doesn't interest me.

RSS: *It doesn't interest you?*
DL: No.

RSS: *What are some of your favorite movies and movie actors?*
DL: Well, I was a great fan of the great days of the French cinema. I think one of the best films I've ever seen is *Les Enfants du Paradis*, terrific I think. I think *Rashomon*, the Japanese one, is pretty marvelous. I'm a great admirer of Willie Wyler, *Mrs. Miniver, Dodsworth*, and very long ago, the old German silent cinema. Funny they're not doing anything much now; it seems to go in waves.

RSS: *What about actors, actresses, do you have any favorites?*
DL: I think my favorite actor or actress is Katharine Hepburn. I've never worked with anybody who combines real gift with immaculate technique like her. She's a very gifted person.

RSS: *Have you ever wanted to work with Marlon Brando?*
DL: Yes, I thought about it once for *Lawrence*; we even approached him over Lawrence. I think he would have been marvelous, but he was doing *Mutiny on the Bounty* at the time.

RSS: *Maybe you could say, just for clarification, what is cutting? A lot of people just don't even know what it means.*
DL: I was fortunate enough to be a cutter for many years. I started off on feature films and then I went to newsreels. I cut newsreels for three or four years and then went back and did feature films again. You learn more in the cutting room, I think, than any other department of the studio because you see all that's being done, you see it there on the screen.

I know when I was a cutter, there were several misconceptions about various people. I must tell you a story about *Lawrence of Arabia*. I was in America in a certain town there, and a lady came up to me and said, "You know, Mr. Lean, I've seen your picture and I think it's just wonderful. What beautiful, beautiful scenery." She said, "I want to ask you a question, were you there?" Now it's incredible, in the same way, when I was a cutter, people used to say to me, "Oh, you're a cutter. You're the one who cuts out the naughty bits, are you?" And everybody thinks that a cutter is somebody who cuts out stuff, which is not the case, of course. He does cut out stuff, but when you sit in the movie theatre, half the effects, whether the audience knows it or not, are caused by the juxtaposition of pictures, and as a cutter you select what the audience shall look at, when. And having shot the film, the film is the material from which you make the finished picture. You've got yards and yards of cloth, like making a suit, and the exact shape it will have depends on how you cut it.

For instance, you can take a simple scene of me talking to you. I would do a shot that showed both of us, all the way through the scene. And I'd do a close up of you and a close up of me. Now what are you going to start the scene on, on your close up, my close up, or the two shot? Three choices. Now you probably haven't got the nerve to start on a close up, so you start on the two shot, so that the audience knows exactly where they are. It might be effective to start on the close up, and it comes to a point where you ask me a question, then I cut to my close up, for the first time, answering it. Now if I've used the two shot, as I said just now, obviously your close up has been cut out up to that point and my close up has been cut out up the point when I answer your question, because the scene's been done three times, once in two shot and twice in close ups, and to that extent one is cutting stuff out but one is not throwing the material of the scene away.

RSS:    *That means the scene is done three times or with three cameras?*
DL:    Three times. You can do it with three cameras, but it is not a good way of doing it.

RSS:    *Television style.*
DL:    That's right, because the photography suffers. Now the interesting thing, to come back to this simple scene we're talking about, of course, it depends a lot on the actor. It depends whether it is more interesting to see a person listening than seeing other people speak. I remember years ago I cut a film called *Pygmalion*, from which *My Fair Lady* has since come, and Leslie Howard was acting in it. He was a marvelous actor. And I know as a cutter it was always very difficult because he was so good at reactions that every time you could have played practically the whole scene on his close up, running the dialogue of the other people on him, he was so good at it.

RSS:     *And how long does the cutting and editing process take after the shooting's finished?*

DL:     On an average length film, I suppose working very hard, three to four months.

RSS:     *Because when you're shooting you probably have an idea at the back of your mind, that positive, you probably know . . .*

DL:     I have a very clear idea, in fact.

RSS:     *. . . that the close up will come out and that's what you have in mind.*

DL:     No, I'll go further than that. In fact, I'd rather go dangerously too far in that direction. On certain things, I think that it would be very good if we played the whole scene on a close up. For instance, in the action scene with the dragoons, I was talking about a riot. There's not actually a riot; it's a procession in the street and it's charged by the dragoons. Now I show the procession coming up the street and I show the dragoons starting to charge and as they hit the people, I'm fed up of these battle scenes of people pulling out swords in close up and, crash, a man gets his head bashed in another close up and that sort of thing. I've decided that as they clash, as the dragoons hit the crowd, I'd cut to Zhivago and I'd just stay on his face for about a minute, just for the sound on it. And then, at the end of it, cut, and there are bodies in the street and the dragoons are gone. Now I've taken myself out on a limb because I haven't shot anything beyond the actual charging down the street, so if it doesn't work on his close up I'm cooked.

RSS:     *I've got just one last question. When you said the theatre didn't interest you, what is the feeling, what is the response that interests you about movies?*

DL:     I suppose I love looking through a camera and I like, I love making compositions. In the theatre I would be in the composition of the proscenium arch. I couldn't alter the audience's viewpoint to my viewpoint. I couldn't put a rectangle round anything specific. I could do a little by lighting, but not much. And I think it's fascinating to go in and say, "Look at that detail," which you certainly can't do on the stage or, at least, I don't think you can.

# David Lean: A Teller of Tales

## MARY BLUME/1970

D A V I D    L E A N  has been called "the world's most wanted movie director" and was recently listed as one of Hollywood's three golden boys, the
other two being Mike Nichols and Stanley Kubrick, a combination that makes
him blink. His recent films have been huge in size yet greatly scrupulous—
Katharine Hepburn, his star in *Summertime*, compares him to both a Medici
prince and a Medici craftsman. He is chronically behind schedule and over
budget, but the money boys, deeply moved by the fat grosses of *The Bridge
on the River Kwai*, *Lawrence of Arabia*, and *Dr. Zhivago*, treat him with awe. He
is, says an MGM representative in London, "a thoughtful and aristocratic
man."

Lean was completing his fifteenth film, *Ryan's Daughter*, which he shot
in a specially built Irish village, except for a side trip to South Africa when
his beach scenes were rained out. Written by English playwright Robert Bolt,
who also did the screenplays for *Lawrence* and *Zhivago*, the film stars Robert
Mitchum as a mousy Irish schoolmaster, Sarah Miles as his young wife, and
Christopher Jones as an English officer, stationed in Ireland in 1916, who becomes her lover. Principal shooting began February 1, 1969, and the gestation
period until release will have lasted twenty-one months.

The technical work after shooting is Lean's favorite part of film-making.
"It's a terrific kick to see the scenes as they were intended." He loves the final
shaping of the film: "It is the God department," he says with a grin. He was
working in England's Pinewood studios—a combination of heavy buildings
and formal gardens so baronial that it has served as background in James Bond
and other films. Hollywood was chosen for some of the final work. "The MGM

---

From the *International Herald Tribune* (October 3–4, 1970). Reprinted by permission of Mary
Blume.

lab in Culver City is the best in the world," Lean says. "It's fabulous. I also finished *Zhivago* there."

Stories abound of David Lean's quests for perfection, leaving the impression that he is a quirky, unrealistic man dreaming the impossible dream at a cost of millions. The impression is wrong and the very word perfectionist makes Lean shudder.

"It sounds so fussy," he says. "I go on and on trying to get what I hoped from a scene. If I know 50 percent is wrong, I go on and on as long as the actors can take it, even if I finally only get 10 percent more. It's damned hard even to get 70 percent of your hopes.

"And there's the awful pressure of time and money. Yes, I do think of the money, I always think of the money, it's like some sort of fruit machine clanking away. You've got to think of the money, otherwise you'd do one shot a day.

"That's why I work with the same people. If a rehearsal's no damn good, I can say to the crew now go off for twenty minutes and leave me with the stand-ins.

In the old days when something didn't work, I'd have complete paralysis. But when I work with the same people I can do as I like. They won't think I'm loony."

Lean is often described as an uncompromising zealot. In fact, the accommodations a director must make are endless, he says. A big problem is casting. "No actor is really right. This one may be too sweet, that one too hard. And then there's the problem of availability.

"In *Ryan's Daughter* Robert Mitchum is a diffident, ineffectual man who is called upon to be strong for the first time in his life. You've got to feel, without the actor acting it, that this is a strong man. If you took a weak man for the part, it would be too boring, so you take Mitchum, who will find the diffident first part difficult, for his strength in the second."

A handsome man with great charm, finely cut features, and, as Katharine Hepburn points out, the world's longest eyelashes, David Lean was using Pinewood studios for work on the soundtrack of *Ryan's Daughter*. The studio bar was full, its sound stages empty, and Lean was having lunch in the vast dining room, vulnerable at a corner table near the entrance.

"David! Do you remember me?" (Fine impersonation of delighted recognition.)

"David! Remember me? You look wonderful—still."

"David! Remember me? I want you to meet my daughter, a budding actress . . . " The budding actress had too much eyeshadow and far too many teeth.

"David! Remember me? Where are you staying? I have this script . . . " ("An anti-war script, no doubt," Lean whispered after the man had gone. "They always are.")

"David! Remember Bombay? Can you still eat Tandoori chicken?" This from an ex-romantic lead grown fat who was to return three times with Tandoori recipes, remarks, and restaurant addresses.

"This place is full of ghosts, I haven't been here for twenty years," Lean said. "I lived upstairs when I was doing *Pygmalion* here. So did Leslie Howard and Wendy Hiller. Now quite honestly, it's gone to pot."

Lean, who won Oscars for *Lawrence* and *Kwai*, lives in Rome and has a left-hand drive on his Rolls convertible. He plans to take a year off after *Ryan's Daughter*. "I always do, it's frightfully hard work and I'm lazy. I usually go around the world one way or another. I adore boats, don't you? Smashing."

Born into a Quaker family in Croydon, near London, David Lean started working in films in 1928 at the age of nineteen. From carrying tea-cups he rose to become a specialist in cutting and was England's top cutter by the 1930s. He also had a thorough grounding in the making of newsreels. He is an enthusiastic still photographer ("sometimes I stop the moviola and say isn't that lovely?") but doesn't want his photographs published because "it's too much business."

He does not think of film technique and his shooting method is, he says, more casual than one may think.

"It's essential to learn to use the tools of the trade, then it's up to talent. Technique is easy—you just lie back on it—the last thing I think about is *how* to shoot a scene. I get the actors right, then I photograph it. I don't say sit there *or* here.

"In a visual sequence like a chase, then I'll work it out precisely, shot by shot.

"The overly technically conscious stuff—it's terribly easy to tilt your camera. As Billy Wilder says, 'We did it all at UFA.'" Lean describes himself emphatically as "not with it" and was angered by *Easy Rider*—"I was angry for the Americans," he says.

The sloppy craftsmanship of many of the younger film-makers irritates him. "It's very hard to tell a story, so they say the story's not important. It's very hard to photograph well, so they say the photography's not important and you get this grainy film. It's very hard to get good acting, so they say we don't want good acting, we want young kids who feel it. Well, you can't *feel* it," Lean said.

His first directing job was Noel Coward's *In Which We Serve* (1942), which was followed by the other Coward films, *This Happy Breed*, *Blithe Spirit*, and the small classic *Brief Encounter*. Lean's cameraman was Ronald Neame and his associate producer was Anthony Havelock-Allan, the producer of *Ryan's Daughter*.

The association with Noel Coward, recalls Havelock-Allan, was especially smooth. After giving them a script for *In Which We Serve*, which took four and a half hours to read and would have taken eight hours to play, Coward left the partners on their own.

"For *Brief Encounter* Noel wasn't in England. In *This Happy Breed*, we'd cable him for one minute twenty seconds of dialogue. Back would come one minute thirty seconds of dialogue with indications of how to cut the extra ten seconds.

"I learned a lot from working with Noel," says Lean, "a lot about handling actors. He is tactful as anything, encouraging to frightened rabbits, tough when necessary."

After the Coward films, Lean went on to make, among others, two Dickens pictures, *Oliver Twist* (seen in the United States in a heavily cut version) and the fine *Great Expectations*. There followed two films with his third wife, actress Ann Todd (he has since divorced and remarried) which were probably Lean's worst, though film buffs are perversely beginning to praise them at the expense of his later work. There are, in fact, attempts to suggest that, of late, Lean has sold out to wide-screen commercialism, but any viewer can see that the intimacy of, say, *Brief Encounter*, remains basic to every Lean film.

"*Kwai*, the first big one I did, was supposed to be little," he says. "I remember saying to Sam (producer Sam Spiegel), 'It's going to look bigger than you think.'

"When Robert Bolt and I did *Lawrence* we thought of it as an intimate story, but obviously one had to have a lot of camels and horses. It becomes an epic." Lean made a face. "I hate that word. It sounds like *Ben Hur* or *The Ten Commandments*."

*Ryan's Daughter* is an attempt to limit some of the problems of size. "Robert and I had done *Lawrence* and *Zhivago*, the one based on history, with the great *Seven Pillars of Wisdom* behind it, the other on a huge novel which would have gone on for twenty-four hours if you'd shot it fully.

"We found ourselves on both of them having to shoot scenes in cable-ese. We got sick of this and were slaughtered by the critics for it—I'd like to see them have a go at it, by the way—so we said let's start from scratch, without a great big thing on our backs, and that's how it happened." He thinks *Ryan's Daughter* is the most completely realized of his films, with *Lawrence of Arabia* in second place.

Before the Tandoori chicken man could bear down upon him again, Lean suggested a visit to the dubbing room, where as many as sixteen sound tracks were to be carefully chosen and blended to be heard behind the scene. The scene he was working on was between Sarah Miles and Christopher Jones and was backed up by a variety of sounds, from a glass being put on a bar to bombs, music, children's voices, and the relentless tapping of the village idiot's foot against the wall. Lean was confident, cheerful and enthusiastic; the bombs, he decided, were too loud, the children's voices too late.

The scene itself was deeply moving, strong and revealing: in a few moments the English officer's past history of shellshock is brought out, as is his relation to the Irish villagers and the desperation on both sides that leads the officer and the schoolmaster's wife to a love affair. The scene, David Lean nonchalantly explains, was written in simply to advance the plot by getting the lovers into each other's arms as quickly as possible.

"David," says producer Havelock-Allan, "is a marvelous story teller, not only of the main scene but of each scene in a story. In another age he would have sat round a fire and told stories."

A word most frequently used about Lean is concentration. Katharine Hepburn, talking about Lean while on location in Spain, says that in her experience only Howard Hughes has an equal ability to concentrate. Havelock-Allan, who also produced *Romeo and Juliet*, compares Lean to the protean Franco Zeffirelli.

"David is Michelangelo, total absorption. Zeffirelli is Leonardo, doing everything—costumes, plays. David is a one hundred percent film man. No, a one thousand percent film man," he said.

# A Lean Portrait:
# An Audio Interview with David Lean

## JOSEPH GELMIS / 1970

(THE FOLLOWING is a transcript of Joseph Gelmis's audio interview with David Lean. The interview was was broadcast over the radio to publicize the release of *Ryan's Daughter*.)

GELMIS:    *Mr. Lean, I was going to ask what you've been doing for a year in the West Coast of Ireland—and this morning you showed me a portion of a reel of* Ryan's Daughter—*and now I know. I know why it took a year to get it. What I saw was exquisite and I almost feel it was something . . . that . . . films like that aren't made anymore.*

*There were cloud sequences there which were just subliminal backdrop, atmospheric kinds of shots—and just took seconds on the screen—which must have taken days and days to shoot . . . Could you just describe, for example, how one went about getting those clouds madly dashing across the beach?*

LEAN:    Well, the whole thing about this sort of game . . . making this sort of picture . . . in which atmosphere is very important . . . is to grab it when you see it. And one day we went down the beach—and I was in a car right up on a cliff—and I saw these clouds racing across, and I just packed up what we intended to do, and went and shot them quickly. Because, you know, in a half-hour they could be gone. And that's it. You can't sit and wait. What we did do was to sit and wait for sun—or for the rain to stop, which it hardly ever did. That's really why the film took so long.

GELMIS:    *Well, the clouds for example: it seemed to me that, I thought, those clouds that were shot coming over the mountains were in fact speeded up—slow-motion*

---

From *Sound on Film* (radio program #10, November 1970).

*shots, time-sequence shots, where you left the camera there and changed the speed. Was it normal speed?*

LEAN:    No. You are very quick and very right. Instead of twenty-four pictures a second, they were shot at one-and-one-half pictures a second.

GELMIS:    *Could you have done that in the editing process?*
LEAN:    No.

GELMIS:    *Is that the shot you got very quickly.*
LEAN:    No. That we did only about three weeks ago, as a matter of fact. I meant it for another sequence and I suddenly thought it would look very good cut in, because I got this shot of the clouds racing across the beach, and I thought it would be rather good having them coming down the mountain and then cut to the beach. On the beach they were moving at the right speed; and over the mountains they were being undercranked.

GELMIS:    *You also used a great number of different kinds of shots on that beach scene where she meets Robert Mitchum as the schoolteacher coming back from a sojourn in Belfast. There were shots, very distant shots, in which there was a zoom. There was a subjective shot when he chases after her and the camera almost seemed to be handheld. It was rolling over the beach and then there were what seemed to be tracking shots, too. And they were all mixed in, in such a way as to—one—fit, and yet, at the same time, give you different emotional equivalents . . . different reactions. Now clearly, your background as an editor made you know which kinds of shots to use, even when you were planning them.*
LEAN:    Yes. If I hadn't been an editor, I think I'd be almost lost. I save a whole lot of mistakes by editing. It's my right-hand technical-man, as it were.

GELMIS:    *There were no helicopter or aerial shots then? That was just a "high-shot" from a mountain or a cliff . . . ?*
LEAN:    No, no . . . Just straight.

GELMIS:    *What kind of equipment were you using to get that enormous zoom-shot of her on the beach, him on the beach?*
LEAN:    A normal "zoom lens." I hate zooms on the whole because, I think, you know you turn on the television and it's nothing but zooms. But I like them every now and again.

GELMIS:    *What place does music play in your movie? Clearly, you have motifs: you had her motif, his motif . . . Where should the music be in order not to be intrusive and at the same time to sort of add something?*
LEAN:    I think that where one gets in terrible trouble is if one just asks for a lot of "Mickey Mouse" music. By that I mean, you say, "Well, I've got a love

scene here; I'd like some rather romantic music; sort of a nice romantic noise." That doesn't work. It's rather like directing actors in a way. I think you've got to tell him what to do. Very often, the music supplies half of the effect so that if you see the film before the music's on it, you might think, "Well, that shot's completely unnecessary."

But with the music, you will see the reason for it.

GELMIS:    *You've worked with Maurice Jarre before?*

LEAN:    Yes. I've worked with him on *Lawrence of Arabia* and *Zhivago.*

GELMIS:    *What is the working relationship in this case? How soon does he get a chance to find out exactly what you are doing? When does he start composing . . . before he's seen the film? Is he on the set?*

LEAN:    No. I think that's generally a waste of time. With Maurice I wait till I've got a "rough-cut"—that is until the whole film's roughly together. And I show it to him and we decide, first of all, very broadly, on what the music has got to do in the picture. And then he will go away and he will write some main themes. He doesn't attempt to fit it to the picture at all. He just plays it on the piano. And it's frightfully difficult to tell, because he'll say, "Well, bum-bum-bum . . . this will be the violins; this will be the drums; and then there'll be a very sad solo horn, I hope, coming in here." And so on and so forth. And then when one's got the picture finally cut and you're not going to make any more alterations, you decide exactly where the music's going to start . . . where it's going to finish. And he's given exact measurements. And he's also given a moviola—which is a little, tiny projection.

GELMIS:    *A one-man projection screen, in effect?*

LEAN:    That's right; that's right. Like a "home movie." And he sits there and he plays the piano to what he's seeing on the moviola. Or, he'll play the piano and record it on the tape-recorder and see how it fits with the picture. And then it's got to be all orchestrated of course. And the absolute nightmare is when one has the first musical session. Then there are anything up to a hundred musicians sitting there—and you literally hear the thing as it's meant to be for the first time. And every now and again I'll ask him to do a slight adjustment. I'll say, "This has an overall gay feeling to it. Can you put in a touch of sadness somewhere?" Or, "Can you make it a little more exciting there?" It's very hard to describe.

GELMIS:    *Does one have to have musical training, or is it just purely instinct or knowing what you like in order to be a director who asks someone to write music for him?*

LEAN:    I can't read or write a word of music. But, I know somehow quite a bit about it, I think. I used to be very tentative about talking to a composer, but now I'm not so.

GELMIS:    *Do you prefer working with the same people as much as possible? Once you've found people you like, like Maurice Jarre? How about the technicians and the people who work with you—the editor, the sound people?*

LEAN:    Always. Always. I try to work with the same people because you cut out a whole lot of mush, if you do work with the same people. They know how you work. I know how they work. I know their "tender corns" and they know mine. And it's much easier.

GELMIS:    *How does that compare with your relationship with Bolt? Are you both strong personalities who get along very smoothly? Do you clash? Do you go back and forth and have to spend a day or two apart writing scenes?*

LEAN:    No. Well . . . we have some pretty heated arguments from time to time. But, by the time we've finished, I don't think there's any scene that either of us disagree with. It's generally . . . the scene is arrived at by mutual discussion and I'd be very surprised if Robert said there was a scene in this film that he objected to—from a writing point of view. In other words, that he wrote anything that he didn't believe in. He may not think I've done it very well; and I think the same very often. But as far as intention is concerned, we agree.

GELMIS:    *Well, very few people—film-makers—are in the privileged and fortunate position that after all these years of working so hard you find yourself in, where you can spend between eight and ten months apparently preparing a screenplay which you cared about and you felt was the right screenplay, as I understand happened in this case for* Ryan's Daughter. *Is that true that you worked all that time in Italy, on and off?*

LEAN:    Yes. We worked for about ten months. But, I mean, it's not being in any special position. I mean, we don't get paid "overtime" as it were. And if we could do the whole thing in a month, we'd get paid the same money.

GELMIS:    *What is it therefore, in the make-up of David Lean that makes him so meticulous? Is it just the need to satisfy oneself when one is very demanding? Is it as simple as that?*

LEAN:    It's a kind of fear, I think. When I say "fear," I'm not *literally* frightened. But I don't want to put anything out that I think I could do better, within reason. I don't mean that I would, given the chance, spend six days in getting one shot. I wouldn't do that. But—I wouldn't, for instance, like to go back to the script. I wouldn't dream of starting shooting a script until I was satisfied that it was the best we could do on paper. Then it's up to me to get it on film . . . It's purely trying to do one's best.

GELMIS:     *Do you find working that long gives you an opportunity to know the characters, so that you don't even have to put things down . . . that there are things unspoken about the characters that you assume about their lives . . . that there's much more of a life even than you have to put on the screen—and that therefore you can convey that to the actors?*

LEAN:     Well, you've got to know the "character," you see. And Noel Coward said to me years ago, a very good thing, I think. He said, "You've got to know what every character eats for breakfast even though you should never show them eating breakfast." And it's very, very good. You've got to know what sort of people they are. Would they do this? Would they do that? As it were, a question of taste with "characters"; it's like knowing a living human being.

If you know them very well, you could say, "Well, I don't think he'd like that"; or, "He'd do this or that in that circumstance. He'd be shy here, or brash there" . . . whatever it may be. And that one learns during the script of course.

GELMIS:     *What was the point of making* Ryan's Daughter? *Why did it give you enough incentive, in working on the script, to want to spend a year, a year-and-a-half of your life, making the movie? What was it about the film that motivated David Lean during this whole time?*

LEAN:     I love making movies. I hate working on the script. It's a kind of necessary chore for me. I'm not a word man. I'm a picture man. And I love getting behind a camera and trying to get something on the screen. I love cutting. I love putting the whole thing together at the end. And I love the job that we're doing now of putting all the sounds together . . . the music, the dialogue, the wind, the waves, and all the rest of it. And it's, I suppose, the greatest excitement in my life—making a movie. And I like taking long holidays afterwards—"recharging batteries," really. Then one's got to find the film and that's frightfully difficult. And in this film, we thought we'd like to write a love story and sat down and tried to do it, and this is the result.

GELMIS:     *In the case of* Zhivago *you started with what is called in the moviebusiness, "a presold property," that is to say a famous book. You start with an original; are the problems so totally different that it gives you more freedom or less freedom? Or is it not a question of freedom? Because, in fact, when you're dealing with* Zhivago *there's known material that people are waiting to see.*

LEAN:     Yes. Well, that's it you see, and that's really why Robert and I decided to do this. Because on *Zhivago*—which was absolutely slain by the critics—it was a very, very difficult job. Because you take a great big book like that, which if you literally filmed the book would run for about twenty-four hours, I suppose . . . perhaps longer . . . don't know. I suppose it would take an average person about four days solid reading to read that book. And we, as it were, chopped it down to three hours. Now it can't possibly be Pasternak's *Zhivago*. And . . . it's a frightful handicap one's in. However one likes the book, one's in its "chains." And so we decided to do something in which we were absolutely free, and we didn't have to have this character doing that or this sort-of person doing something else. We decided we would do it absolutely on our own and cook it up from the start. And so, in away, it's a much, much greater freedom.

GELMIS:   *Are you a terribly romantic person? I know the word doesn't have as much cachet today as it might have had in Hollywood, say in the thirties or forties and even through the fifties. But the sequence I saw today was enormously exhilarating . . . romantic . . . and I say this without trying to make you feel good. I thought it buoyed me; it pushed me up in the air. It was an enormously romantic sequence, and the music and the scene and the sequence and everything else all fit together.*

*And Zhivago, one remembers, has a great romance set against an historical background. Where does this come from? Why two films in a row now? What is it in you at this moment in your life or career or whatever that's responding to this particular kind of métier?*

LEAN:   Well, it's very difficult to say because romance has become a rather dirty word and because it has, I suppose, now-a-days a connotation of being untrue . . . of putting sugar on a pill . . . and so forth and so on . . . too much sweet. I don't think this is—If you ask me why I'm romantic, I think I can only say that I enjoy life. I love life. I've had some marvelous times. I don't want to die. And I suppose I tend to put some of the wonderful things of life on the screen. I want to put them on the screen. I think the excitement of a love affair is hard to beat. And in this film we've tried to do that.

It's also about temptation—about a girl who marries a man and then has an affair with a much younger man. And I think it's a pretty true story of these terrible poles—the "animal" which is only a little way under all our skins, which can be very exciting but very dangerous.

GELMIS:   *Well, she wants "something more." She's not satisfied with her portion, which makes her a romantic in a sense, because she's unwilling to settle for things. She always wants something outside of immediate, limited range.*

LEAN:   Well I suppose it's like all of us, especially when we're young. We expect that there's going to be some wonderful something or other. We don't quite know what it is. And that is what this girl is after. And she marries and it's a kind of disaster, but she won't give up believing that there must be something better. There must be something there—not this rather dull, good husband of hers. And as I say, she meets this young man and finds this excitement. It's also her disaster, but she finds it alright.

GELMIS:    *Where did you get the people to play these parts? How does one go about finding the right people, since obviously, they're going to add or detract from the script, from your vision?*

LEAN:    That's always very difficult because like almost everything in movies it's a compromise. And what Robert and I do is—we finish or we get a very good idea of the character, various characters and then we start saying, "Now I wonder if this person would be good, or that person. No, so and so would be very good in this part, but they probably haven't got enough sense of humor." And then we'll think of another actor and we'll say, "Well, on balance I think he would be good." And then you'd get hold of the agent and say, "What about Mr. X?" And then he says, "Oh, I'm sorry, Mr. X is busy." And so generally you end up with the actors that you did not think of in the first place. Sometimes you thank your stars that you didn't get the actor that you thought of in the first place. It's a matter of luck, really.

GELMIS:    *Once you've got them how do you bring out or how do you coax out or how do you give them that opportunity to do what it is you want them to do?*

LEAN:    Well, I think one works differently with different actors. Some actors need a lot of encouragement. But I'd better backtrack a minute. You see I haven't known an actor or actress, a good actor or actress—who hasn't got tremendous nerves. And one part of my job is to soothe those nerves and give them confidence. It's no joke going up there in front of a camera. You know I even find it talking to you with this microphone pointed at me. Now if you'd also got a lens pointed at me I couldn't sing as I sing in my bath. I'd be cooked! And that is certainly true of every actor I've known. Now some of them will become much too quiet and nervous and you have to pull them up. Others will try to overcome their nerves by bluster and you have to pull them down. My job really is tickling their talent. And there are various ways of doing it with different people. Of course, they all vary.

GELMIS:    *How about in Mitchum, or how about in Sarah Miles? They're two totally different kind of people.*

LEAN:    Sarah Miles is intensely interested in the part—concentrates and very easy to work with. Mitchum? He's been at it a long time and if I may guess at it, I would say he despises being an actor. So he covers that up with a certain amount of bluster and talk. And it takes a bit of time. This film—I think it's probably one of the best performances he's ever given. He took a little time to get into it.

GELMIS:    *How much artifice does one bring to natural surroundings? For example, I think a lot of moviegoers are being surprised to see reflectors and lights in a bright sunlit situation. Did you use a wind machine, for example, on that beach in order to knock their hat off? At one point both their hats go off.*

LEAN:    Oh, there's always artifice, because, I mean a whole film is artifice. Nothing's real. The great thing is to make it appear real, of course. You saw a scene where Mitchum's hat blew off. Well, of course one couldn't ask God to blow the hat off at that particular moment, so there was a nylon thread attached to it, so off came Mitchum's hat! Sarah Miles runs after it, and of course the real wind took her hat off. And I cut it. I said, "Cut." And after I'd cut it, I thought, "Well, that's rather good—her hat blowing off too." So we picked it up again and she went running after his hat. He picked up her hat and they exchanged hats—and it was quite charming. But that was absolute accident.

I'll tell you the funny thing about shooting location pictures. Because you are there, it's very easy to forget to shoot the long shots. Now that sounds absolutely mad but I've known it to happen many times when I was a cutter. People, for instance, go out on the beach and they see this huge beach and they photograph various shots and they forget that the camera hasn't photographed what they have been seeing all day long. And so every now and again it's very necessary to show it, damn great long shot, you know. But you've got to be very careful that the background doesn't become the foreground. And people, of course, are the foreground.

GELMIS:    *How detailed a script is it, that you work from? For example, that whole sequence where there are footsteps, where she's walking barefoot in his footsteps and then suddenly the sea comes in—she's left standing there—and when the sea pulls back, the tide pulls back, his footsteps are gone . . . She has lost her way. It's a metaphoric kind of thing. It's a subliminal sort of thing that just . . .*

LEAN:    Absolutely planned. It's a picture of a young girl, very excited, going to meet a man—and as they're walking towards each other—you expect them to throw their arms around each other, but instead of that he takes off his hat and says, "Rose" and she says, "Mr. Shaughnessy," and you realize that it isn't that position at all—that she is mad about him, but he doesn't know it.

GELMIS:    *How much after you had shot the film did you find that you had to rearrange? Are there such things as emotional curves or dynamics?*

LEAN:    No. It worked. For better or worse, there it is. We had him meeting her on the beach and it was all very nice and "airy-fairy." Now what we wanted to say was that she's all very physically attracted to him and so we got this idea of a big close-up of his footprints in the sand and after a moment her naked foot comes in and treads in them. At the end, a wave comes up and engulfs her and she's like a sort of tight-rope walker, sort of swept away by these erotic thoughts of hers. We didn't want to make it too, oh, "beautiful, sweet young thing" you know. She's not such a sweet young thing—she's got a lot more in her than that, as we all have.

GELMIS:     *Would you use people in a film who you did not like, but whose ability you admired or are all actors in a David Lean film extensions in some way or another of his own personna—because he in some way identifies or is simpatico with them?*

LEAN:     I don't like to admit it really, but I suppose it is true. Because if you work on a script and you're partially responsible for cooking up the characters, I suppose that all those characters are in fact an extension of one's self. I don't know what Robert would say about this, but I think they must be. I mean, I think that's where a really great writer must have quite a time of it with himself. Just imagine Shakespeare—"I know a bank where the wild thyme grows" and the most hideous human doings. He must have them all in him.

GELMIS:     *Don't we all?*

LEAN:     Not to that extent, surely. I suppose a great genius—Beethoven, I suppose—I should think they have a pretty difficult time.

GELMIS:     *People like Norman Mailer, incidentally, who put their films together, and John Casavettes, as supposedly a self-analysis group-therapy/exploration, finding out "who they are" in the process of making the movie—obviously are dealing, are using people who are in one way or another facets of their own personality because they're using their friends and they're going about and making, in effect, a home movie—a very expensive home movie.*

LEAN:     I think they should make home movies—because, perhaps one is that interesting, I don't know. I think one's got to fight out all sorts of private battles with oneself, hasn't one? One's got to be a "can carrier" or one's a bore. I don't think one can unload everything on one's friends, in this case, an audience. Maybe it's interesting—I don't know. I don't really go along with it though.

GELMIS:     *Well, what is your function as a director then? To be a tastemaker or to be a problem-solver or to be a story teller . . .*

LEAN:     Oh, to be an entertainer. They pay a lot of money to go *see* a movie, and I would agree with Billy Wilder who said, "The first law is not to bore." . . . to give people an interesting evening.

GELMIS:     *If you had a chance to rewrite any chapter of your career or your life right now, would you—would you do it?*

LEAN:    No, in my career I've been terribly lucky. I came in in the very early days of silent films. There were no unions and because there were no unions I had the chance of going around doing all sorts of jobs, from making tea, turning the camera, going into the editing department, being an assistant director, and at one time even being a wardrobe mistress. And it was a wonderful background. I could move around. Now you can't move around like that. I suppose you can in the new film schools. I think it's terribly important because if you're aiming to be a director you've got to know the tools of your trade. And I don't know how that is done now-a-days in the picture business because you either become something to do with the camera department or the sound department or whatever it may be, but it's frightfully hard to get a good all-around grounding.

GELMIS:    *What was the big opportunity that somehow gave you your chance?*
LEAN:    When I was a cutter I became a kind of film doctor in which they would give me films which they thought were very hard to cut or had been cut by somebody else, not too successfully perhaps, and I would put them together and apparently did quite a good job. And I started at this time getting various offers to direct small pictures and one of the wisest things that I ever did was to say, "No." Because I knew at that time there were lots of very cheap—they were called "quota-quickies." They were made by the Americans for a pound a foot, and you didn't have a chance. If you made a film in three weeks and it's a disaster nobody says, "Well, he did it in only three weeks; he had lousy actors, lousy cameramen." They all say, "He's a lousy director." Nobody remembers the time. It's the same now-a-days. Everybody's very happy if you come in on schedule, but if the film's a disaster, they don't say, "Well it was a disaster, but he came in on schedule." They say, "It's a stinking film." And anyhow, to go back—in those days Noel Coward was going to make a film called *In Which We Serve*, which was about the Navy. And he looked around because he had never done a film before. And he asked all sorts of people and several of them came up with my name, and so he offered me the co-direction job with him on this film. And, of course, I jumped at it, and it was a success, I'm glad to say. And he was very generous. He was really bored by film direction. He liked writing and acting best, and in the end he said, "Well, you can take anything I write and make a film of it. What would you like to do, dear boy?" And one of the outcomes of this was *Brief Encounter*.

GELMIS:    *Did you feel panic with the first film? And is it a feeling that have never left you, in terms of approaching each new film? Do you feel panic right now with* Ryan's Daughter *coming up within a month or two months of opening?*

LEAN:    Well, no, I don't feel panic. I've done it now, for better or for worse. When you've spent a lot of money as I have on this, you get panic about the public and the critical reaction. On *Zhivago* we had about the worst critical reaction I've known; certainly the worst for me. Then, gradually, word of mouth got around and people started going to it, and it turned out to be a huge success. And I get panicky about that. I mean if the critics dive into this and tear it to shreds, will people come? I think they'll probably like it. I think it's the best film I've done. And I just hope it will run long enough for the word of mouth to get about.

GELMIS:    *Mike Nichols spoke of panic when he made* Catch 22. *He said, "I felt that way when I made my first film. I feel that way now, and I just don't know how to overcome it."*
LEAN:    You always do, always do . . .

GELMIS:    *He said, "It's always like the first time and I don't know how to change that particular aspect of it."*
LEAN:    Every film is, as it were, a prototype. So you begin with nothing in your hands, as it were. Most people, they've got a business which is built up on solid blocks and when they take on their next job they add a bit to the block. But with a movie, you start absolutely from scratch and it's very frightening. I find the first two weeks I do on a movie pretty bad. I mean, as far as result is concerned, I'm over-meticulous. I worry too much. After a few weeks the film starts to take over in a way and I find it easier to know where to put the camera, how to talk to the actors. It all starts to gel, and then it's just a matter of luck. Oh, it's not so much luck, it's how good the script was, and of course, you have no idea until the public see it what the film is like. I mean this reel I showed you just now, I didn't want to bring you in there because I'm ashamed of it. I thought it looks absolutely horrible.

GELMIS:    *I'm glad to hear that. You mean there are better things even to look forward to?*
LEAN:    Oh, yes. It's one of the worst reels in the picture, really. But it's always difficult starting and I suppose directors are just like actors. They have to pretend a bit more perhaps. No, that's not true. I suppose we all pretend that we are more confident than we are.

GELMIS:    *But you have to because you have a hundred people standing around looking at you and wondering, "Is he going to pull it off? Is it going to be another juggling feat today?"*
LEAN:    And that's one of the wonderful things about working with people you know. One of my great, great panics was being on the set and running a

rehearsal, seeing a rehearsal, and something that you didn't bargain for crops up and an idea you thought was good is no good and you cannot think how to do it, where to put the camera or whatever it may be; and a kind of mental paralysis sets in. Well, now because I work with the same people. I say, "Look, I'm completely lost. Have some tea. Go away." And they don't go away saying, "Oh, what an idiot!" They think, "Thank God for a cup of tea!" And off they go. And as soon as one's calmed down a bit, you know, the idea comes. But it does happen quite a lot.

GELMIS:   *Doesn't a creative person have to dry up? I mean, you can't every day be the same person you were the day before. You can't always have the juices flowing. You can't have the same disposition you had the day before. How does one either discipline oneself, or does one just take a day off, or does one . . .*
LEAN:   No, you can't take days off . . .

GELMIS:   *. . . or does the work suffer . . .*
LEAN:   Yes, it does, I think . . . I think it depends on . . . I mean, one of my great problems is tiredness. You have to keep on and on and on and towards the end of a long film you get frightfully tired. Because making a big location picture is a great physical strain, and you just long to have a couple of days off and sleep. And you can't. And you've got to try to keep that energy going. I think the whole thing about this entertainment business is energy, vitality.

GELMIS:   *It sounds like training to be a boxer. It sounds almost like getting ready for a fight or a match.*
LEAN:   It is rather. It is, in a way, isn't it, with everybody—athletes, actors? I'm always saying to actors, "Run up that dynamo." Because although you may be sitting stock still in a big close-up, just reacting to somebody else talking, if you really got that dynamo running, and really concentrating—it'll come boom out on the screen. And if they are thinking of nothing, you will see they are thinking of nothing. And it's a question of energy.

GELMIS:   *Are you able to sleep at night when you are working, or do you have to take a lot of pills or do you just not sleep?*
LEAN:   Like a log.

GELMIS:   *Do you have final cut in a contract or does any director really have final cut in a contract, or is it always subject to the president of the company saying, "Now, look, we're going to have to do this or that or the other thing?"*
LEAN:   No. I have final cut.

GELMIS:   *In your contract?*
LEAN:   Yes.

GELMIS:     *You must be one of the two or three. I think Mike Nichols may have had it. The American critic Pauline Kael has written a 60,000 word, I understand, introduction to the re-printing of the republication of the* Citizen Kane *script by Herman Mankiewicz, I think it was. And it hasn't come out yet, but I understand from somebody in publishing that it's a refutation of the whole "auteur" theory and also sort of a put-down in a way, by using that, of Orson Welles, because it says that the script was so detailed and everything that has been credited to Welles, whatever that means, is now seen to be the work of the screenwriter of the screenplay, that, in fact all he had to do—he could have in effect, sent in a very talented hack and he could have put that thing together.*

LEAN:     Well, I'd like to see the so-called author come and put it on the screen, and I'd bet there'd have been a fine old hash. Why isn't he the famous director that Orson Welles is? Orson Welles has an enormous talent. I'm sorry, it's so over every frame of *Citizen Kane.* You can see he's a great director. And I'll bet he also had a lot to do with the script. It's so fashionable now-a-days to tear down these big people.

GELMIS:     *Why couldn't he (Welles) have "made it" though? Obviously, he had this enormous talent. Is talent alone not enough?*

LEAN:     I don't know. It's very impertinent of me, but I would guess that Welles has probably too much talent—in too many directions.

GELMIS:     *Well, I thank you very much, Mr. Lean. I wish you well.*

# Lean at SF

## CATHY FURNISS / 1971

AT THE RETROSPECTIVE of David Lean films at the San Francisco Film Festival that director said, in reply to a question, that he *does* intend to do another Charles Dickens film and that it will be *A Tale of Two Cities*.

Asked how he goes about choosing music for his films he said: "I like music. I take a lot of trouble with it. You move differently when listening to music. The whole thing with music is how you place it. Robert Bolt and I plan it in advance. We decide music will start *here* and end *there*. I wanted to use "Bless 'em All" for *The Bridge on the River Kwai*, but the royalties were too expensive. From my boyhood, in the first World War, I remembered "Colonel Bogey," had crude lyrics, so I thought we'd better whistle it. I never dreamt it would catch on."

Does he find it easier to work with men than women? "No, I like women. A couple of films with men and you get typecast."

Asked who were his favorite actresses he said Celia Johnson and Katharine Hepburn, and added that the latter was not only gifted by nature but the possessor of "superb technique."

Peter O'Toole was chosen for *Lawrence of Arabia*, Lean said, only after many actors had been considered and Albert Finney had turned the part down and that: "We were getting desperate. One day I saw the film called *The Day They Robbed the Bank of England* and there was O'Toole. He is taller than Lawrence was but he is a good actor and a good actor can make a character seem more real than the actual person."

Asked his opinion of cassettes: "I love a whacking great screen. Small screens require a lot of cheating. Cassettes are the poor man's movies. Sure we could

---

From *Films in Review* (April 22, 1971). Reprinted by permission of Roy Frumkes Productions, Inc.

make a movie on 16mm film, and even cheaper on 8, but it would be no damn good. I don't mean to be rude about cassettes."

About *Ryan's Daughter:* "Bolt and I decided to write the screenplay ourselves and to make a compassionate film. Novelists can be more detached than film-makers, for with films you're 'nose to nose.' We wanted to show a woman in the optimum balance between expectation and reality."

Asked to describe just how he and Bolt collaborated: "Working with a writer is like working with an actor. It's a slow process of talking. I never say yes to something I don't believe in. Bolt and I finally agree on everything that goes in the script."

Why did he cast Robert Mitchum for the schoolmaster in *Ryan's Daughter*: "Always cast against the part and it won't be boring."

Does he like to improvise? "No. I don't believe in it. None of the arts, at their best, are improvised. Consider a Beethoven composition, or a Hepple-white chair."

Does he like critics? "Critics know little about the technical aspects, but perhaps that's not important."

His next film? "It will be called *Gandhi.* The whole of Asia will be down on us."

# In Defense of David Lean

STEVEN ROSS / 1972

Q:  *What do you consider to be your best film?*
LEAN:    It's an awfully hard question because I think one always tends to think that the most recent film is the best. I think *Ryan's Daughter* has come off in relation to what we've tried to do. You know, I wished all my films had the bloom of age. *Lawrence of Arabia*, for example, got torn to bits by the critics and now on its reissue in London it's making more money than it did when it first came out. It has passed through the envy belt. It's now an old picture. Nowadays everybody's flocking to see it. When you make a new film, especially today, I think everybody's there with their knives out, waiting. And we really stuck our chin out because we've made, as it were, an old-fashioned picture. I've made it as smooth as I can. There are no jump cuts, the photography is as good as I could get it and there's no improvisation . . . it's all written in the script. So obviously we're in a difficult situation. There'll be a lot of crosscurrents, which I can't forecast.

*Ryan's Daughter* is a very explicit, understandable film, and perhaps we've occasionally made a point only too well or too explicit. Critics, of course, only give you the benefit of the doubt when you are obscure. Let me tell you a wonderful story that really happened to illustrate what I mean. If projectors are not synchronized, the academy leader, showing a countdown from ten to one, may appear over another scene. At a show in London, not all that long ago, this disaster happened, and the numbers were superimposed over a dramatic scene. The critics fell over themselves with enthusiasm over these numbers which really didn't mean anything, but made the whole thing seem so significant.

---

From *Take One* (no. 22, 1971).

Q:    *A few years ago on American educational television Sam Spiegel said that he'd brought you into* The Bridge on the River Kwai *very late in the game, that he had the script, heard you were in Hollywood without a project, and simply assigned you to the picture. Yet the film's crew is obviously yours: Jack Hildyard on camera, Malcolm Arnold as composer, and Peter Taylor as editor, all these people had worked with you in the past. Could you give us the genesis of your involvement with* Kwai?

LEAN:    I came to New York for personal reasons. I was damned near broke, because you never get any profits out of film—you know that. It's a sort of fantasy. If you have an enormous film that just falls over itself at the box office, then you'll get something, but I hadn't had anything to date like that, and an agent came along to me and said there was a man called Sam Spiegel, who I remembered years ago in London before he was at all well known, and he's got a book. He gave me the book and I read it. I saw the agent a few days later and said, "Look, if the script (which he didn't have) is more or less faithful to the book, then I'll do it." Then I couldn't get the script. When I finally read it, I said, "If this is it, I don't want to do it. I'll start again from scratch but otherwise I'm out." I mean the whole film when I read it started in an American submarine; the thing was being depth-charged. It really was not very good. So we started all over again, and, one writer, two writers, three writers, and including me, four writers worked on it, and we finally did it.

Q:    Ryan's Daughter *is an often depressing and doubtful film that culminates in a pessimistic vision of life which permeates much of your work to date. In* Great Expectations *Miss Haversham asks, "What have I done?" and in* Bridge on the River Kwai *Colonel Nicholson literally repeats the same question. In* Ryan's Daughter *everyone seems to be asking, "What have I done?" Everyone's trying to help each other and everyone is hurting each other without meaning to. It seems a very trapped situation.*

LEAN:    We tried to portray a girl who had romantic dreams. Her romantic dream then came to her, and we portrayed the love story between her and Chris Jones in a purposely over-romantic way, almost like an erotic dream . . . very, very much in her head. And we hoped that if we stopped the film in the middle of the love story and asked the audience what is going to happen to their love, they would say "it's burning far too bright to last." We certainly made it intentionally over-romantic so that the girl would have a frightening fall back to earth and realize that her heaven does not indeed exist.

Q:    *You no longer receive actual screenplay credit for your films, yet you are still a very active participant in the creation of your films' screenplays. How would you describe your contribution during this phase of the filmmaking process?*

LEAN:    I spend so much time on a film's script not because I consider myself a writer, but because I consider it my homework for directing the film. So, when we start the film, I know a great deal more about the characters than the actors who are portraying them do. Now, half of my job is to explain those characters to them if they don't get it off the written page. This frequently happens. And people often ask me, "Do you have temperamental fights with actors?" No, I don't. Because most actors, in fact nearly all the good ones, are basically frightened rabbits. It's quite something to stand up and be photographed. Just think of a snapshot, how difficult it is to get a snapshot of your friends. Immediately, that tiny little camera somehow freezes them. Now add microphones, lights, a whole crew, plus dialogue, and it is a very frightening thing. I remember reading once an essay by Max Beerbohm, who tried to answer why actors, actresses, and opera singers take criticism so personally. He said that it is because they personally are being criticized. It is *their* face, *their* voice. While all of us can say, "Well, we wrote a bad script that time, or a bad book, or a bad piece of music," we can retire from it, but *they* are up there on the screen. I have an enormous respect for this fear, and a lot of my job is to give actors confidence. I was telling someone the other day, who was rather surprised, that I often have the camera turning on what they think is a rehearsal because they'll have an ease they won't have if they know that damn box is turning.

Q:    *You have always given a great deal of time and care to the music used in your films. Since you began your collaboration with composer Maurice Jarre however, you've come in for a lot of criticism for his somewhat overemphatic scores. There is a scene in* Ryan's Daughter *in which the suicidal British officer and the village half-wit are walking together along a beach at sunset. There are explosives on the beach. Your staging of the scene brilliantly milks every bit of tension from the situation and sensitively brings out the thematic linkage between the two characters which is so important to the film. But Jarre's loud and obtrusive music telegraphs in very crude terms everything that you had gone to such great pains to establish visually.*

LEAN:    I understand your objections to the music there. I'll tell you, this is what happens. You see, you get frightened. I personally didn't think that Chris Jones put over the fear of those explosives. I mean, it should be an exciting scene, you should be thinking that at any moment this bloody half-wit is going to blow the whole damn thing up. So, I asked Maurice—again, my fault—"put 'danger' into it." Now if you'd seen it without the music, I think the scene might not work. I know you pay a price by saying, "Well, it's corny, that music," but I'm not sure, I wasn't right. I don't know . . . you know, it's awfully hit-and-miss. It's certainly my fault. It's lack of confidence, you know. You see a thing so many times, and you get frightened.

Q:   *If you look at films like* You Only Live Twice *and* Battle of Britain *it is hard to believe that Freddy Young photographed them, at least when they are compared to the work he has done for you. [Young has photographed every Lean film since* Lawrence of Arabia.*] Have you noticed this difference, and if so, why do you think he's always better when working for you?*

LEAN:   Yes, I have sometimes noticed this difference. I would think it's simply because I give him an intention. The whole thing in movies, whether it's sound, photography, or acting, is intention. An actor can be absolutely helpless if he doesn't know exactly what he's supposed to be doing. Sometimes we'll be having trouble, and I'll go off with an actor and ask what's wrong. Invariably the reply will be, "I don't know what I should be thinking when he's doing this or she's doing that," and I'll say, "So and so, so and so, so and so," and I'll give him a whole list of thoughts, and he'll say, "Thank you very much," and suddenly come alive. It's the same thing with a cameraman. You know, you come in here and suppose you are Freddy and you have to photograph this. Now if I say, "Set up the camera over there and photograph it," Freddy will set up some lights and photograph it perfectly well. But supposing I say I would like us here on stage to be photographed in brilliant light and for the press that was in the audience earlier to be lit with ominous shadows, well, Freddy will latch on to the idea and give me something far beyond that. Now that's an awfully simple example, but I would say that it's intention that helps.

Q:   *You were in emphatic disagreement earlier today with the woman who felt that the kind of extensive training and apprenticeship which you had before becoming a director is no longer necessary for the neophyte filmmaker.*

LEAN:   She thought it was possible for someone without extensive training to make a first rate commercial film. I don't think it is. Obviously, there are some people who can do it . . . I mean, Orson Welles did it with *Citizen Kane* when he was only twenty-four, but mind you, he had that wonderful cameraman Gregg Toland to help him on the technical side. I don't believe in having no training. I don't believe it's true for any of the arts, and I suppose we're inching towards an art.

# Adventures in the Dream Department

## JAY COCKS / 1984

AGAINST THE ADVICE OF HIS ASTROLOGER, who had warned that it was not an auspicious day to travel, Victor Banerjee left Calcutta for New Delhi—on the ides of March—hoping for the role of his life.

In the hotel lobby, a producer, reckoning with Banerjee's chain-smoking, thought it politic to mention that the director had sworn off cigarettes. Banerjee, with copy of the *Passage to India* script in hand and struggling to manage, besides, a whole portfolio of dreams, began to appreciate the merits of a smokeless interview.

The man who made *Lawrence of Arabia* opened the door of the suite, and Banerjee saw at once what everyone immediately notices about David Lean: the strong, handsome lines of the face, the certain set of the jaw, the strength. And the eyes, glistening blue, that never look away. "Eyes like the sea on a cold day," an actress said long ago, adding quickly, "but not the Mediterranean."

Banerjee thought of everything he wanted to say and ask about *Lawrence*, and about *The Bridge on the River Kwai, Great Expectations, Doctor Zhivago, Oliver Twist, Brief Encounter, Breaking the Sound Barrier, Ryan's Daughter*, and all the rest; all that he could tell the director about buying the cheapest seats in the cinema so he could afford to come back and see the films over again; all that he could thank him for. But he remembered he was calling about a job, and under such circumstances, compliments can be veiled solicitations. So he said a simple hello and stepped into the room.

Lean spoke idly, about the pollution that would make it impossible to shoot a single scene in Delhi, about a trunkful of manuscripts that was, somehow, adrift in the Victorian vastness of the Taj Mahal Hotel. Banerjee struggled to keep up his end of the chat. He was dying for a smoke, desperate to talk about the script. He summoned his courage and brought up a scene he partic- ularly liked. Lean seemed pleased, but changed the subject. Banerjee excused himself and sneaked off to a bathroom for a smoke. A few quick puffs, then he threw the butt into the toilet. It would not disappear, not even after repeated, thunderous flushings. Banerjee went back to the director. What will he make of my absence, all that incredible noise? The director wanted lunch.

There was no script talk during the meal, nor did there appear to be any imminent when they returned to the suite. After six hours and insufficient nicotine, Banerjee broke and blurted, "David, am I playing Dr. Aziz?"

"Of course you are," David Lean told him, and when Banerjee said. "But you haven't *told* me," told him again. Then it all came out. Everything, about every movie and even about smoking, about craving, just at this moment, a single cigarette. "What bloody nonsense," said Lean. "They're always mak- ing up silly stories about me. Please, my dear boy, smoke to your heart's plea- sure."

It was the first direction Victor Banerjee got from David Lean and, like most of what was to follow, he was grateful for it. He lit up, and both men talked for a long time more, about the script, about the character of Dr. Aziz, even about the mutability of astrological portents. Lean reached for Banerjee's script and wrote in it, "March 15th. Victor: A good day for travel. David."

In film history, there have been few voyagers as adventurous as David Lean. He is fearless in his choice of subject matter—whether it be a world-classic novel or a history-molding life—and he is absolutely fixated on having his way with it, on getting it right. "He's totally devoted to cinema," says another for- midable British director and former Lean colleague, Michael Powell (*The Red Shoes, Peeping Tom*). "Once he's agreed to do a film of any kind, I can tell you you're going to have a rough ride until it's finished." "He really is a perfection- ist," says Lean's friend Katharine Hepburn, whom he directed in *Summertime*. Then she adds affectionately, "He doesn't care if everyone dies around him, he'll just take over the camera, prop up the actor, and get what he wants. Un- derneath it all, I think that David knows how ridiculous he is, how absolutely impossible he can be in his search for perfection, but he just can't help it."

It is remarkable how close this fond description of Lean comes to a sketch of the foursquare Colonel Nicholson played by Alec Guinness in *The Bridge on the River Kwai*, a man whose grand dreams of glory turned into dementia and destruction. Odd, too, that for a director who says, "I'm not a brave man, not a courageous man, not at all," success should come from what seem, outward- ly, to be celebrations of courage, daring, and recklessness but that are, more deeply, films founded in turmoil and ended in uncertainty, melancholy, and the hard presence of unshakable fate. Lean's masterpiece, *Lawrence of Arabia*

(1962), has the sweep and size of a great adventure film. It is about a poet who wanted to be a regent, a scholar playing at warfare whose exploits, through Lean's eye, take on the shimmer of legend as seen through a veil of heat. Some heat is blinding, but here, for Lean, it becomes purifying. Yielding up a vision of a man out of time, fighting to find himself and losing, in the confusion and compromise that follow, all hope of self-knowledge and all chance of redemption.

*Lawrence* was a major popular success and it won seven Oscars. *Kwai* did as well but was narrowly understood, either as a bang-up war flick or as a muddled antiwar tract. Nearly thirty years after its first release it looks, perhaps even more clearly today, to be one of the definitive films about war, certainly the most implacable. It is comic, almost ruthlessly so, elegant in the way it arranges and compounds its narrative ironies, pitiless in its portrait of war's grand follies. But it is a film of heroic size, and Lean strikes a perfect balance between the folly of heroism and the heroism of folly. He is brave enough to show that war is madness, but that there is a terrible beauty *in extremis* as well, and that men can respond to it, dying grandly as they die in vain.

"I don't know any director who doesn't go down on one knee whenever *The Bridge on the River Kwai* or *Lawrence of Arabia* is discussed," says Steven Spielberg. "I feel a great deal of reverence for David Lean. I think he has a much broader movie vocabulary than a lot of directors, including myself. He's the last of a generation of classical artists as picture makers, he and Kurosawa." Lean's sixteen films in forty-two years have earned forty-five Oscar nominations, including six for his directing. His films have almost always turned a profit, often substantial, sometimes astonishing. (*Doctor Zhivago*, the director's biggest popular success, has brought in more than $200 million worldwide at the box office.) He has always enjoyed the respect of his peers and now enjoys that of the younger successors to the tradition of the well-made film.

What's wanting is consistent critical favor. "I can't remember the last time I got a good notice," Lean says wondering and a little wounded. He can still quote from a savaging visited upon *Lawrence* by the then critic of the *New York Times* and claims that "after *Ryan's Daughter* I had such terrible notices that I really lost heart." His faith may be partly restored by the warm reception of his newest effort, but the fact remains that after *Ryan's Daughter* Lean did not make another feature film for fourteen years, partly, he says, "for lack of subject" and partly, one suspects, out of wounded pride.

Lean is not vituperative about critics. He saves his scorn for the "money obsessed" studio executives who offered to back *Passage* if there was an explicit rape in the cave or if the young Adela, not the aged Mrs. Moore, could meet the attractive Dr. Aziz in the moonlight at the mosque. But, he says, "the critics are the intellectuals. I'm always frightened of intellectuals. I think one tends to take the critics too seriously, but you can't meet the general public, and if your mother tells you the movie is great, you say, 'Yes, very sweet of you, but you would.' The only people who really don't give a damn, who are out there giving their opinion are the critics. They are the only people, as it were, you can believe."

This sketch of the cinema press has a surprisingly sweet naiveté that is colored by yearning. Lean's films are epic journeys of disillusioned self-discovery, and he himself has traveled widely. Ask him about his travels, and the names pour out like whistle-stops in a dream: "I've been through the Panama Canal twice, been to New Zealand, the Cook Islands, Tahiti, the Tuamotu Archipelago. I've sat on top of Mount Cook in a helicopter, had two Boston whalers docked out in French Polynesia, one in Bora-Bora and one in Rangiroa, which is my favorite place in the world." But one also recalls Michael Powell's remark that "he's very cloistered in his life" and Katharine Hepburn's perception that "David understands loneliness. He understands passion. He understands desperation." It would take just such a man to sound so wistful about his bad press, a man who, having become one of the world's great film makers, had still not got over being young and without palpable promise, being, as he says, "looked on as a dud, you see."

Lean was born seventy-six years ago in the then comfortable London suburb of Croydon, the elder of two brothers. His parents, both dazzlingly handsome in family photographs, were Quakers. "This upbringing . . . ," muses his friend and frequent collaborator, the wizard production designer John Box. "David's got this puritan English passion that is very intense. Passion and ice." Lean was early set apart, shadowed by his younger brother, Edward Tangye, who was "very clever," and by being a Quaker, which kept him out of the local school. "It was Church of England," Lean recalls, "and wouldn't have me." Religion also discouraged moviegoing, but he heard all about Charlie Chaplin from the family charwoman, Mrs. Egerton. She acted out his comic exploits, "running around the table, skidding around the corners," while David sat dazzled in the basement kitchen. When he was thirteen, while attending the Quaker Leighton Park boarding school, he started to sneak out to the neighborhood cinemas on Wednesdays and Saturdays. The first film he saw was a version of *The Hound of the Baskervilles* made in 1921—and the movie did not disappoint. "That beam of light traveling through the smoke," he recalls. "It had an immediate magic for me." It was a magic that seemed impossible to touch. "I never thought I would have the luck to go into films," he says. "They were in the dream department. I think they still are."

In the real world, his family had begun to fall apart. "I wasn't very close to my brother or my father," he says now. "My mother was a sweet woman, rather pretty. My father was tall, and I think he was handsome. He wasn't a stern character. He left my mother. I must have been in my early teens. It was sort of a bad part of my life, really. My father, poor man, plagued by guilt. It was a difficult thing in the best of times, but in those days, and being a Quaker, you can imagine. He didn't get married again, He went off with somebody else. She was a nice woman. I got to know her later. I think he was a sad man. I don't really want to talk about these personal things."

His father Francis sent Tangye to Oxford, but Lean did not attend because "my father didn't think that would be worthwhile. It did hurt my feelings, but that's as it was." David—"hopeless" all through school—was outfitted with black striped trousers, a bowler and a brolly and sent off to work in the accountancy firm where his father was a senior member. He used his fingers, as he still does, to count everything, and he lasted a year.

Just nineteen, he cadged a job at London's Gaumont Studios, where his first responsibility was to fetch tea and load film for the camera department (salary: 10 s. weekly). Showing a flair he had previously displayed only in the school darkroom, Lean quickly graduated to "number-board boy" and, finally, to "third assistant director." He befriended a studio projectionist—"I still remember his name: Matthews"—who let him watch the day's rushes from the projection booth, peering down from near the source of that beam of magic light traveling through the smoke. One day Matthews was screening "some cut stuff," film that had been assembled, rudimentarily, by an editor. Lean, who knew that the scenes had been photographed hours apart, was fascinated to see them put together seamlessly. "I thought, 'What a magician's trick.' It was a new language." He began to cut, and quickly became fluent. He edited newsreels at Gaumont British and British Movietone—using scissors directly on the negative—and graduated to features, where he got fired from an early assignment by Producer Alexander Korda for overcutting. "It was," Lean says now, "a very good lesson."

And well learned. By the late 1930s, he was the bright young man of the business. "Everyone was stunned by the marvelous editing he did on Gabriel Pascal's *Pygmalion* in 1938," Powell remembers. "Those scenes of Wendy Hiller learning phonetics were created by brilliant editing." It was also, as Powell points out, editing done in a highly unconventional way; Lean, as the industry buzz went, "cuts talking films on a silent head," meaning simply that Lean used a silent editing machine to cut sound movies. "He cut what he wanted to see on the screen," Powell says, "and to hell with the sound, leaving the poor assistants to pick up the sound track. The visual was the essential. David constructs purely in terms of images, using the material the way a composer might use a theme."

By the time he came to work with Powell on *One of Our Aircraft Is Missing* (1941) and *The Invaders* (1942), Lean had already been offered films to direct, but he waited for the right assignment. That turned out to be Noel Coward's prototypical piece of brave-it-through wartime propaganda, 1942's *In Which We Serve*. Lean co-directed with Coward, who provided two pieces of advice, "One: don't pop out of the same hole twice. Two: do what pleases you and, if what pleases you does not please the public, then get out of show business."

Posterity ought to thank Coward for omitting critical admiration from the prescription, but even if he had included it, Lean would probably still have hung on. Film for him was not just a calling; it was a lifeline. "If there hadn't been film," he says, "I don't know what I would have done. I think I would have been a pretty good failure." Film seems to be the very source of his strength, and, if he cannot fully expect those who work with him to share his obsession, he demands at very least their unflagging commitment. He tends to float away during the infrequent social occasions that occur while he works. "I do become obsessed by a movie, in a sort of maddening way, I must say," he confesses. "I get a close-up of somebody superimposed over the soup." It can be unnerving to intrude. "David's greatest virtue is his enormous concentration," says Sam Spiegel, who produced both *Kwai* and *Lawrence*. "He's deeply engrossed in what he's doing and has an *idée fixe* about anything he does." During the shooting of *Passage*, Lean was on a hillside, admiring a fine sweep of country, when a member of the crew approached him. "Isn't it beautiful" Lean said. The crew member allowed as how, after months of shooting, he was sick of India and wanted to get home. "Then." said the director, "get your ticket and go, if that's what you want. You should work in a factory."

Sign on for a David Lean film and all else becomes secondary: social contacts and marriage contracts. Lean is not awash in friendships. "He doesn't know too many people," Hepburn says, "and he's also a shy man. But to me he's a dear friend, endowed with every virtue." Eddie Fowlie, a prop man who has worked on the Lean team since *Kwai*, has sometimes got the director's hand-me-down automobiles, and recalls, "After *Zhivago*, I think, I got a telegram to do something for a Hollywood company in the south of France. But David said, 'Don't go. I've got more money than I know what to do with, and you're the best friend I've got . . . share it with me.' But I told him I had to feel like I was earning it." It may be worth noting that, though his friendships may seem movie connected, his marriages have not survived the film assignments.

Lean, who has a son from his first marriage, "was not the sort of man that husbands are made from," said his third wife, British Actress Ann Todd, at the time of their divorce in 1957. "Too tense, too mercurial." "David and his work are more important to him than I am," said his fourth wife, Leila Devi, who

met the director in 1954 and divorced him in 1978. "Life has only one meaning for David—his film making. I never talk to him until he talks to me, even
if he's just tying his tie. If I speak, it startles him."

The couple drifted apart, and Lean met Sandra Hotz in India in the late
1960s, when he was checking into a hotel owned by her parents and she
showed him to his room. Lean who approaches interviews on such matters
with all the relish of a man who is about to have root-canal work performed
with ice tongs, is genuinely surprised when mention is made of her brief appearance as Mr. Fielding's wife in *Passage*. "Who told you that?" he wants to
know. "I had been trying to keep it a secret. I met my wife in India. I don't really want to go into it." Reports Katharine Hepburn: "She's a good wife . . . one
worth waiting for. It takes a lot of props to make a tower and you can't have
two towers. Sandy and David have a marvelous life, creating, traveling all over
the world. She's very much a part of the art."

Lady Lean—the director was knighted this year—performed extensive li-
aison work during the making of *Passage* in India and was by her husband's
side five years earlier for what he calls "the biggest regret of my whole career,"
when a long-cherished dream went smash. Lean wanted to make the best
and fullest account of the Bounty saga. Says he: "Captain Bligh is a much ma-
ligned man. I think he was a terrific chap, though he had no sense of humor.
Christian was a young man who just got swept away by the South Seas." Lean
and the peerless scenarist Robert Bolt (*Lawrence of Arabia, Doctor Zhivago*)
wrote feature length scripts for two interrelated films. The first was to end
with what the director calls "the fantastic voyage of Captain Bligh in the open
boat across the Pacific to Australia"; the second was "the search by a terrible
man called Captain Edwards for Christian and his men." Lean says the scripts
are "the best I've ever had."

Lean likes to quote a Hindu proverb—he nearly put it into *Passage*—that
says, "In very simple terms, we're like a leaf on a river and we've got a very
small paddle. We can go this way or that way, but only minutely. We're on
that damn river and we're going to be taken down it to some destination." The
*Bounty* did not make it into the water. Robert Bolt had a stroke. Producer Dino
De Laurentiis came to Tahiti, where a full-scale replica of the *Bounty* had already
been constructed, and announced he did not have the money to go ahead with
the movie. Lean fought with his old friend John Box about the scope of the
project; Box left within hours by motorboat. "It was horrible," he says now.
"When you're very fond of someone, you can hurt them. He and his wife were
on the pier when my boat pulled out, and he pretended not to be looking. The
two of them were fading smaller and smaller, and finally I saw his wife break
and run back up the hill. It was like the ending of a David Lean film."

Some feared the *Bounty* episode might put an end to his career. Composer Maurice Jarre, who has scored all of Lean's films since *Lawrence*, saw him at the time of the debacle, and says, "Something inside him had died." "I wonder," said Rod Steiger, after finishing work on *Doctor Zhivago*, "just how much of that man is alive when he is not working." *Passage* pulled him back, and together, again. "He became younger and more dynamic," Jarre says. "He got back that very sparkling light in his eye. Something was really much more alive in him."

And kicking, it might be added, with all appropriate animal energy and stubbornness. Filled with joy at his first sight of the Marabar Cave location, Lean grabbed his camera and, according to Eddie Fowlie, "went up that granite mountain like a bloody hare. That rock must be the biggest monolith in the world, and David went up backwards on his ass." Lean had what he calls "tiffs" with Judy Davis and Alec Guinness. Lean and Guinness have wrangled on and off since *Kwai* when the actor wanted to play Colonel Nicholson more comedically and the director, in every sense, set him straight. "I have a great fondness for David," Guinness says, "but the atmosphere on the *Passage* set was overly tense. And we did have a dust-up concerning the small dancing scene I had. The dancing was nothing great, but I had rehearsed quite a bit for it, and then David didn't even come round the day I did it. He said he never liked Indian dancing anyway." (The dance, which was scripted to end the film, has been eliminated in the final version.)

Judy Davis mixed it up with Lean "mainly at the start of the movie—for about two months. It was like two bulls locking horns. I don't think he trusted me because I was new and young. It was a matter of winning his respect." At the outset of filming, Victor Banerjee found himself locked in combat with the director over an appropriate accent for his character. The actor did not want to play an "obedient English sheepdog." That argument lasted for four days, and Banerjee's speech preference prevailed. He offered his hand to Lean, who responded, "What the hell for?" He shook hands the next day, however, and on the last day of principal photography, when Banerjee brought off an especially tricky scene in one take, Lean came from behind the camera and embraced him.

Throughout *Passage*, there is a sense, ironic and unapologetic, of mortality. "I'm not a Quaker now. I don't know what I am," Lean says. "I don't think, as Mrs. Moore says, that it's a godless universe. But I wouldn't know what God is. We're still trying to find out, like plumbers trying to mend Swiss watches, what makes us tick." *Passage* certainly offers no answers, just images against the void, like Mrs. Moore turning at night in a room, sensing something and, at a distance, down at the river, a crocodile flipping the rippled moonlight with its tail. Moments like that one work at a primal level that only true artists can reach. "David is a director who really sees the images in considerably clearer terms than any other director I know," says Sam Spiegel. "After looking at each inch of film thousands of times, I still get an added surprise at what's on the screen." Pressed on this, Lean, arming himself with a wide safety net of qualifiers, admits, "I've just begun to dare to think I perhaps am a bit of an artist." He has "had thoughts that *Passage* might be my last movie," and also confessed to its cinematographer, Ernest Day, that he has only just begun to comprehend what films are about.

This is understandable in a way. The director who cut from an extinguished match to a desert sunrise in *Lawrence* has a gift that almost passes understanding. "In one cut," marvels Spielberg, "he creates the entire scope of the Arabian Desert."

*Passage* and *Lawrence* are linked by their last lingering images: a woman, alone, at a rain-streaked window; a soldier, lost, obscured behind a dusty windshield. Lawrence is going home; the woman is already there. But both have been changed fundamentally, uprooted and unsettled forever in a way they never were by the steady mutability of travel. Lean, who has had several homes over the years, has never lived long in any of them. "I sort of traveled in a car and put my clothing in a case and wandered around," he says. "It's a wonderful thing, you know, going to strange places." He lives mostly in hotels or on locations, wherever the movies take him. He has ordered up an elaborate residence for his wife and himself in London's newly fashionable East End dock area, but the Leans have not yet moved in. He is, he admits, "a romantic," and his heart will never be at home. It can be found in any direction, but it will always be away. He lives at a distance, a singular address for the movies' greatest poet of the far horizon.

# Epic Dialogue

## DAVID EHRENSTEIN / 1984

FIVE YEARS AGO, the faculty and students of the AFI spoke with Lean shortly after the release of his latest work, *A Passage to India*, in 1984. The director spent an afternoon at the institute, where, after a screening of *Passage* he spoke openly about his work, his life and his vision.

QUESTION:  *Since we are here with young men and women who have a passion to make films, they have, as one says, caught the fever. When did you catch this fever?*

LEAN:   I was brought up in the suburbs of London. I hated them. I was also brought up in a rather strict Quaker family. I wasn't allowed to go to the cinema. We had quite a big house—a kitchen and a basement—and we had what was known in those days as a charwoman, somebody who swept the floors and did the rough work. She was called Mrs. Edgerton. Mrs. Edgerton was absolutely mad about the cinema and, as I wasn't allowed to go, she used to tell me about it. The thing that really first hooked me was when she told me about Charlie Chaplin. She used to imitate Charlie Chaplin very well by running 'round the kitchen table and skidding and twirling the cane. I used to roll around with laughter. I remember saying to her once, "When they talk, what happens?" And she said, "Oh, it comes up on the screen in writing." I said, "Well, that must look ridiculous." She said, "No, it doesn't. It works." That's when I first got the bug.

When I finally was allowed to go to the cinema, one of the first films I saw was Douglas Fairbanks in *The Mark of Zorro*. I'll never forget the sword fights and the villain grasping his head, taking his hand away, and there was a huge Z on his forehead. It was magic to me. If you knew what the London suburbs

---

From *American Film* (vol. 15, 1990). Reprinted by permission of David Ehrenstein.

were like, you will understand—it was very, very gray, and the movies were a journey into another world.

I was absolutely hopeless at school and when I finished—I was just nineteen—my father said, "You better come into the office." I went to this damned office in the city of London with a bowler hat, striped trousers, and black coat as a chartered accountant. Awful. I stayed there for about a year. One day I went home, and my mother—my father had gone some time ago—and my mother said, "Oh, Aunt Edith was here this afternoon. She said, 'I don't see any accountancy magazines here. I only see film magazines. Why doesn't he go into the movies?'"

I was overawed by movies. I thought they were so wonderful, literally a dream world. I never thought one could go into them. I applied to a place that is now a television studio. I said, "I'll do anything, carry tea, anything." They said, "Well, we'll take you on for two weeks. If, at the end of it, you seem to be promising, we'll take you on at five pounds a week." And they did. I remember going into the camera department first of all. I remember going up to an old Bell and Howell camera and saying, "What has that done?" And they said, *Roses of Picardy.* This is a film I'd seen—silent, of course. And I remember touching their camera. I couldn't believe that this was the source of all the magic, you know.

QUESTION:    *In your early days, did you work as an apprentice to a master director or learn on the job or? . . .*

LEAN:    I worked with some good people. Yes. I was very lucky. I think the great thing is to work—try to sacrifice everything to work with good people. If you're lucky, a bit of it rubs off.

QUESTION:    *Your relationship with playwright Robert Bolt is legendary in the industry. Will you talk about how you work with him?*

LEAN:    Well, Robert once said, "By the time we're finished, we don't know who got what idea." When we work together, I don't think there is any competition, and quite honestly, I cannot remember very clearly who's thought of what. I'll give you one example. There's a cut I rather like in *Lawrence*, where he lights a match and says, "The trick is not minding that it hurts," and blows it out. Robert wrote this scene. And next there was a scene played in the desert at sunrise. I said, "Look, Robert, I don't quite understand what you're at." He said, "Nor do I, really, but I always think when somebody blows out a match, the ember that disappears is somehow the red of the sunrise." And so out of that, I kind of put it in film terms. Robert hadn't actually written a film script before. It was the first one he had done. I don't think I'm very good with words, but I feel as if I'm swimming in my own water with pictures. And it's that kind of combination.

QUESTION:     *Could you tell us how you use the camera to achieve those painterly images that tell us what's important in a scene?*

LEAN:     Well, you know, it's a terrible job, making a selection on the screen, isn't it? A painter can do all sorts of things to bring up the image he wants people to look at. We are faced with photography. One of my greatest helps is the focal length of lenses. I start with a fairly wide angle, with everything very much in focus, and I gradually up the focal length so that I'll end on a closeup of somebody in which everything is a blur except the eyes of the face. And I use that again and again to choose what the audience looks at, because I try to take an audience by the hand and say, Come look at this. See that man sitting down at that table? He's being watched by a girl.

QUESTION:     *Could you tell us about the conception and execution of Omar Sharif's entrance in* Lawrence of Arabia?

LEAN:     On the mirage? I was out there on the mudflat, and another Jeep was miles behind us. It came over the horizon, and the Jeep, I must tell you, looked much better than the camel because the dust went up in the air behind it. Wonderful V shape, like an airplane in some wind tunnel. And I thought, What a wonderful entrance. Then some people said (and I'd heard it before) that you can't photograph a mirage. So I got out my camera, and I got the Jeep to go farther away again, and I took a series of pictures. And it did come out. That's all there was to it.

I can't bear second units, and on *Lawrence of Arabia*, Sam Spiegel got three. I was mad about dust devils. I thought we were going to have some in the picture. So to one of the units, I said, "You just go out in the desert and wait for dust devils." They got very tired and very sleepy but they got one.

QUESTION:     *In films such as* Lawrence of Arabia *or* Bridge on the River Kwai, *characters such as T. E. Lawrence or Colonel Nicholson seem to be almost symbolic of all that may be thought of as the worst in British character . . . they're very curious people but they're very contradictory. Is there any deliberate attempt to do that in your film?*

LEAN:     No. I'm just interested in nuts. [Laughter] I think they make very interesting characters. When we were doing *Bridge on the River Kwai*, Alec Guinness said, "Now, tell me about [the character]." I said, "Well, Alec, if we were having dinner tonight, he'd be a bit of a bore." He said, "A bore? You are asking me to play a bore?" Never tell actors the truth. [Laughter] And we fought pretty well all the way through that film. Lawrence is a fascinating character. This Oxford don on camelback—I mean, it was absolutely nutty. Sort of intellectual, with a gang of Arabs on camels, you know. Peter O'Toole was very young in his career, and he could have done it better later.

QUESTION:   *I read somewhere that Peter O'Toole was not your first choice for Lawrence. Could you talk about the casting?*

LEAN:    It was a tough part to cast. The first person we went for was Albert Finney. He was very young. I spent four days doing tests with him. He decided he didn't want the part. And I said, "Why?" He said, "Because I don't want to be a star." I said, "Why don't you want to be a star?" He said, "Because I'm frightened of what it may do to me personally." I said, "I can only talk to you as a director. If you succeed and do become a star, it will give you good parts, the best parts." Anyhow, that may not have been the whole story. Maybe they wanted to put him under contract for Christ knows how long. But he went. I also thought of Brando. In fact, talked to him about it. I think he would have been wonderful, because *there* is a secretive creature. I think he's one of the greatest screen actors in the world. I think he's terrific. Hasn't had many good parts. I think he'd have been very interesting. And then I saw the film called *The Day They Robbed the Bank of England,* and Peter O'Toole was playing a sort of silly ass Englishman fishing. Anyhow, he got the part.

QUESTION:   *Could you talk a little bit about how you have worked with various actors?*

LEAN:    Dangerous subject. Well, it's intensely personal. I always try not to speak in a loud voice when I'm talking to an actor on the set. I gently take them aside, and I whisper because I don't want to give the impression, for their sake, that they are being told to do this or that by a teacher. I try to suggest things to an actor. I try as hard as I can to make *them* suggest something that I want them to think of.

The trouble with actors is that it's a very, very difficult job, with this damned glass eye looking at them all the time. It's quite difficult talking to all of you here, but I'd rather talk to all of you than I would have a 100mm lens pointing at me. It's so concentrated. It's part of a director's job, I think, to get the actor to give as good a performance on the stage as he gave to himself in the bath in the morning. So I try to relieve them of their inhibitions. I try to get their confidence. I try to give them confidence.

I can't bear some actors, the rambunctious type who think they know everything. You've got to knock them down and make them realize that they *don't* know everything. If you've really done your homework on the script, you, the director, know the part better than any damned actor, because you've been at it for months. I've had lots of actors who want to change dialogue. I stop them doing it. I won't have it. They took on the script, and they stick to it.

I'm terribly tempted to tell you a rather long story about Sessue Hayakawa. You know, I find constantly that actors really are not interested in anything but their own parts. We had a scene in *Bridge on the River Kwai* where they had all the troops lined up in front of them, and Sessue gets up on the soap box and talks. We went through a rehearsal, and I said, "What's wrong?" Because it was the speech and yet it wasn't the speech.

I write very detailed shooting scripts, because I try to think of how it's going to look on the screen and describe that in the script. And I put down, Close shot, Colonel Saito, so much dialogue, close shot to Colonel Nicholson, listening. Long shot, the soldiers, close-up Saito.

What Sessue had done was to learn all the lines that were only his. He had cut out all the lines that were anybody else's. I looked at his script. It marked the pages in which he spoke. He had thrown out all the rest and had bound it all together. Now, we came to the scene at the end of the picture. Alec Guinness is looking over the edge of the bridge, and he thinks he sees some wires. He goes up to Saito and says, "Colonel Saito, there's something rather peculiar going on. I think we better go and have a look." We walked off toward the bridge which leads down to the rocks, and Sessue stayed there like a rock. I said, "Go on, Sessue, follow him." He said, "I follow him?" I said, "Sessue, this is where you find the wires and where you get killed." He said, "I get killed?" [Laughter] He had thrown it away because he had no dialogue.

QUESTION:    *Did you think of any parts, specifically, for Alec Guinness?*

LEAN:    Yes. [Laughs] The part of the priest in *Ryan's Daughter*. It was a heck of a part. I've had various tribulations with Alec. He's a convert to Catholicism. And he wrote me two or three pages of things that would have to be altered for him to play the priest. So I said, "Thank you very much for being so frank," and then gave it to Trevor Howard.

QUESTION:    *How do you keep somebody from being sentimental?*

LEAN:    Sentimental? Well, I try to avoid saying to an audience, Nudge, nudge, isn't this touching? If the scene is really good, you don't do that, do you? And I try to be very truthful about things in that way. I don't like sentimentality, but I love big emotional scenes. I think one of the best emotional scenes I've ever seen is Willy Wyler's in *Best Years of Our Lives*, where Fredric March comes back at the end of the war. And he goes to his house, and the door's opened, I think, first of all, by a girl who's obviously his daughter. And she opens her mouth, and he puts a hand over it, and then a boy appears, and you gradually become aware of the bottom of the longer passage, of a door, and you also know that the wife is behind that door, because she's the other member of the family, and then she comes out. It makes me choke even now. He's a master at it. I think it's because he has a wonderful heart. He had a wonderful heart, Willy. I loved him.

QUESTION:   *I'd like you to talk a little about adapting a novel. We saw* Great Expectations *last night. So many people have adapted—unsuccessfully and some successfully. And you have made films out of a number of such significant novels.*

LEAN:   I think the thing is to not try to do a little bit of every scene in a novel, because it's going to end up a mess. Choose what you want to do in the novel and do it proud. If necessary, cut characters. Don't keep every character and just take a sniff of each one. When we were going to do *Great Expectations,* we thought that we were completely incapable of tackling such a master as Dickens, and so we looked around and asked, "Who really is an expert at Dickens?" There was a lady novelist called Clemence Dane in London who had also written several plays, and she was sort of a Dickens expert. She did a script, and it was absolutely awful because she did just what I've said. We said, "It's no good." And I said, "Let's have a go." I got the book and quite blatantly wrote down the scenes that I thought would look wonderful on the screen. What I did was try to join up those scenes and write links between them. Of course, you have to have a narrative.

QUESTION:   *You always have the most interesting characters in your film in the foreground, like Mrs. Moore in* A Passage to India. *How did you decide to give her that much interest?*

LEAN:   Mrs. Moore is a wonderful part, and I'll tell you the interesting thing. Have you seen Peggy Ashcroft before? No? That's it, you see. She's very, very well-known in England on the stage. And she's a great stage actress. And we always said, I wonder what the Americans will say? Because here you see an old lady—we're exactly the same age, actually—who is a very accomplished actress. In England I don't think she would have quite that additional impact that you got. In part [her impact] is due to this wealth of experience. She can do it off the back of her hand, I can assure you.

QUESTION:   *How do you perceive her character in the film? I didn't quite understand the scene when she was at the caves and you cut to the process shot of the moon and then the fuller shot of the moon. I realized something mythological was going on, but I couldn't pinpoint exactly what was happening.*

LEAN:   Well, I'll tell you what I was trying to do. I don't think it succeeded. You see, in the book, Mrs. Moore is a very religious lady. Hence, she wears a cross, and in the mosque scene at the beginning, she says, "God is here." And when she goes to those caves, [author E. M.] Forster says, "Those caves were sealed before the coming of the gods, before the coming of man . . . " and so forth. In other words, they were a kind of vacuum when the world was made, and then, I think his expression is, "Man grew curious and drilled a hole." And Mrs. Moore loses her faith in there, or her faith is badly shaken.

Well, thank you very much—put that on film! So I had her come out, flop back in her chair, look at the moon, have the girl come up. I had her put on dark glasses because I was going to put everything from the moment that she put on the dark glasses seen through a strange color so all her POVs would be strange. We failed in the special effects, and I dropped that, so she in fact puts her glasses on for nothing. But I thought that that space and the surface of the moon, with the line, "Like most old people, I sometimes wonder if we are passing figures in a godless universe," was the best effort I could make at saying that her faith was shaken.

QUESTION:    *You seemed to really take your time in telling the story, yet it keeps our interest. I'm thinking particularly of the scene in the monkey temple. Could you talk about pacing?*

LEAN:    I just obeyed my instinct. It had to be slow because a mood is slow, isn't it? I always imagined that girl had lived in a sort of vicarage, brought up in very proper surroundings. And I wrote that scene because in the book she's a bit of a stick. And then there was this question of an assault in the cave. I wanted to prepare the way for it being possible. I wanted to have a scene where a rather prudish girl becomes aware of her own sexuality. Now, this has got to be done slowly.

There was a wonderful place in India where I went about thirty years ago. It was discovered by a couple of men who were tiger shooting, and they got into some thickets and realized there were some statues there. They realized they were erotic statues. These were all overgrown with creepers. Today it's a very nice little park. All the statues have been cleaned. I was there for a week with a camera just shooting photographs. We reproduced it. It's a complete fake in the film. We built statues in plaster, put fake creepers around them, and the art director, John Box, stuck them up against the background of trees in various places. And then we built a sort of platform for monkeys. I had her push her way through on a bicycle, had lots of shots of her, shots of statues, shots of monkeys and so forth, and it's just a cutting job, really. That temple only exists on film.

QUESTION:    *What advice can you give us in terms of staging large crowd settings? Most of the directors we've talked with have never done the huge spectacles that you have done.*

LEAN:    The most important thing, I think, is to get people's enthusiasm. If you say, "When I hold my hand up, you cheer," they'll cheer. Or, "When I put my hand there, fall down on the ground," they'll fall down on the ground. It's no good. I get on a microphone and try, as simply as I can, to describe what the scene is and explain what I would like them to give the camera. I try to give them a feeling that they're contributing to something. The Indian crowds were simply wonderful. They're the best crowds I've ever worked with. Very, very emotional. I'd do one take, two takes, probably print take three, which was the end of it. I'd say, "Cut." And I would applaud them. And they would applaud me, and everybody applauded everybody, and that was the end of the shot.

QUESTION:     *This is kind of a gush but I'd just like to thank you for making* Passage to India. *It sounds like you had to put up with a lot to do it.*
LEAN:     How sweet of you. That's no gush. Yes, well, we did. Nobody wanted it, you see. We came over here because the only people who put money up for films are the Americans. One studio said they'd do it if we put in an explicit rape. And that, thereby, ruined the story, of course. And another person—not American—wrote what he thought was a fascinating memo to me—he wrote words to the effect, "Our audiences are young people. Young people are bored by old people. Cut the old dame."

QUESTION:     *As a director, what's the difference in working on a large-scale picture and a more personal drama?*
LEAN:     If you are on a picture that is just a large-scale picture with no personal drama, it's no good. The whole thing in the big picture is to try to keep the personalities up there in the foreground except when you want the background really to take over.

People often ask me about doing big location pictures. And I'll tell you a funny thing: Most people forget to take the long shot. On *Lawrence of Arabia*, they sent a second unit to the Suez Canal. There was a shot of a double—or we had taken the close-ups of Peter O'Toole, but over his back—across the canal, with the man on the motorbike yelling across the canal, "Who are you? Who are you?" We got the stuff back, and I said to Sam, "Where's the long shot? It's got to have a long shot of the canal."

QUESTION:     Brief Encounter *has always been one of my most favorite pictures. Do you ever have a desire to do a more intimate, small-canvas picture like that again?*
LEAN:     When I can no longer do a big one, yes. Well, as a matter of fact, you know, I've tried to do it in *Passage to India*. That's very much the play of characters—these wonderful characters of Forster's—and the attempts of people to reach each other and go out across barriers. A lot of that is quite intimate, isn't it? Willy Wyler said to me once, "I don't see why anything shouldn't be told through a love story." And he could do it.

QUESTION:     *Do you feel you've changed as a director from the beginning of your career to now?*

LEAN:    I think, probably, I have just a little more confidence. I think a little bit of confidence either makes you unbearable or much better. It's a very funny thing about getting old—you don't feel it. You feel exactly the same. So I really don't feel any different than I ever did, but as I say—and I mean it very lightly—I have just a bit more confidence, perhaps.

QUESTION:    *What is your relationship with the cameraman? How do you tell them what you're looking for?*

LEAN:    One curious thing about cameramen is that they very rarely read scripts or they read them and then forget them. One of the best cameramen I've ever worked with is Freddy Young. He'd always come up to me and say, "Now, look, this is the scene after they've found the baby's dead—or whatever it is." I'd say, "No, Freddy, that's at the beginning." He always got it wrong. What I generally do with cameramen is remind them of the script, and I tell them the mood I'd like to create. I did *Brief Encounter* with a very good cameraman called Bob Krasker. And we started *Great Expectations* with him, and it was almost the same as *Brief Encounter*, very real looking. And I said, "Bobby, much more daring. Huge, great black shadows. Great big highlights over the top, because that's Dickens." And he couldn't do it. And I got him this ex-operator of mine who'd only done a bit of a picture before, Guy Green. I remember these shafts of light coming down, and it was simply wonderful. And he got the Oscar for cameraman on that picture. It's rather like casting actors, in a way. You've got to cast people who have a love for the atmosphere.

In *Doctor Zhivago*, there was a winter scene, a series of scenes in winter, and I wanted spring, so we went to some daffodils. We were growing these damned daffodils for weeks. The scene before was the scene of the family in a small room, and I said, "Come on, let's make it absolutely colorless." Freddy said, "It's going to look bloody awful." I said, "Doesn't matter. It's going to look much better in a minute when we go to the next scene." And we took out every bit of color we could. We even got a spray gun and sprayed some of the colors gray. Now, that scene, which was flat and gray, made the daffodils because of the contrast, of course.

I often think we are only at the beginning in making movies. I don't know what's going to happen. We've got sort of basic techniques, but I think we've got a long way to go. We haven't begun to use all sorts of things. I think we just photograph what's there rather than *making* what's there. That's why I like really doing sets as opposed to real streets.

QUESTION:    *I'm fascinated by your use of sound, particularly at the end of* Bridge on the River Kwai. *Could you talk a little bit about how you shoot the scene in terms of sound?*

LEAN:    I try to write sound and music into a script. I try to describe what I hear in my imagination. I'm always telling the sound people, "Don't be too realistic with sound. The audience has got to think it's realistic, but use it like an orchestra." And I try to do that. That's all. . . .

QUESTION:    *Can you talk about the collaborative nature of the medium and the way you convey your vision to all these people who have to create it?*
LEAN:    When I finish a script, I get everybody in the different departments and have endless cups of coffee with them. Just talk, talk. And then they'll start coming up with ideas and bouncing back and forth. I think directing a movie has got to be a very selfish job in a certain way, because the more a movie is one person's point of view, the better. The greatest thing in acting or in a movie is intention. I'm sure of that. Any fool can go on and take long shot, medium shot, over shoulders and close-ups, and then throw it at the cutting room. I could do that, and it's an easy way of doing it. I do it sometimes when I'm lost, but only when I'm lost because I think in doing all those shots and not knowing quite how it's going and throwing it to the poor editor, you lose intention.

With good actors, you could, if you wanted to, stop them in mid-stream and say, "What are you thinking about?" He or she would tell you exactly what they were thinking about, because film acting is purely thinking. That's why I hate using doubles even in long shots. Celia Johnson—my goodness me, what an actress she was—she was wonderful. Unfortunately, dead now. In *Brief Encounter*, we had a scene in which a man had asked her to come to an apartment. She said she was married, and she said no. And she catches the train, she gets into the train, has the door slam and, as the whistle blows, she gets out, gets onto the platform, the train starts to move and she decides to walk towards the exit. And I just had one hell of a great long shot of this small figure . . . walking up the path. And she walked, she half ran, she stopped herself, and I said, "Celia, that was wonderful. How do you do that?" She said, "Well, she would, wouldn't she?" And she was just thinking of it: I can't wait to meet him; I shouldn't go. And I bet you she could have told every thought passing through her mind. And I think that's the great thing with a script. Try not to get sidetracked. What is this saying? It's saying that. And if you can do that, you'll be the stronger for it, in my experience.

# I'm a Picture Chap

## HARLAN KENNEDY/1985

*Inside every Lean movie there's a fat one trying to get out.*
—Old Hollywood proverb

D A V I D   L E A N   has spent fifty-five years in the film industry trying to live down his surname. Was ever the son of austerely named English Quakers so given to pathological gigantism? Did ever a former clapper-boy, cutting-room apprentice, "wardrobe mistress," and assistant director realize—on such wall-to-wall scale—his dreams of directorial grandeur?

In the last thirty years Lean movies have come ever more vastly built and budgeted, and with ever vaster breathing spaces between them. Five years each between *The Bridge on the River Kwai* (1957) and *Lawrence of Arabia* (1962), and then three between *Lawrence* and *Doctor Zhivago* (1965). Five years between *Zhivago* and *Ryan's Daughter* (1970). Now fourteen years between *Ryan's Daughter* and *A Passage to India* (1984). The mind boggles at the age Lean, now seventy-six, will be when by mathematical progression, he is ready to make his next film.

The shade of E. M. Forster must be casting sympathetic sighs Lean's way. The novelist's own travails in writing *A Passage to India* (ten years, including a break midway to write his homosexual novel *Maurice*) were almost as momentous as Lean's own in reaching the starting line on his longest cherished book-into-movie project. Yet, insists Sir David (knighted last summer), "I would rather make one good picture in three years than make four others in the same time." Who could doubt it? Who could fail to be impressed by it? In a British cinema stuffed with oddball loners—Michael Powell with his hothouse romanticism, Robert Hamer with his gallows farce, the myth-seeking

From *Film Comment* (January/February 1985). Reprinted by permission of Harlan Kennedy.

modernism of Nicolas Roeg and John Boorman—Lean's oddness is less outré but no less provocative.

In the beginning was the clapper-boy, and to the clapper-boy the cinema was God. One can describe almost in a straight line Lean's early, brisk rise—devoid of any hint of Brobdingnagian things to come—from manning the clapperboard for Gaumont Pictures (he quit his father's accounting firm for films in 1927, aged nineteen) to becoming a writer-editor-commentator for Gaumont British newsreels to editing feature films (*As You Like It, Pygmalion, One of Our Aircraft Is Missing*) to his co-directing baptism on *In Which We Serve* (sharing credit with Noel Coward) through to his own early movies, from the forties' Coward and Dickens adaptations up to *Summertime* in 1955.

The plum puzzle at the heart of Lean's life story is this: How can a man spend a twenty-year apprenticeship learning the editor's craft of concision and precision, of slicing the fat off films, and then evolve into a director who seems allergic to using scissors on his films at all? Whatever happened to Lean the lean?

In 1942 Noel Coward, lips pursed and eyebrows akimbo, clipped out advice to his co-director on *In Which We Serve*: "Never pop out of the same hole twice, dear boy." And though Lean has popped out of the same hole twice, of course, from time to time (two Dickens films, two Celia Johnson stiff-upper-lip epics), he has never popped out of the same hole three times. It's the mixture of judicious repetition and sudden spectacular direction-changes that makes Lean hard to pin down.

Even in his young days as a snipper-together of unconsidered footage, working in the primeval dawn of the editing art ("There was no moviola," Lean has said. "You just ran the film through your fingers and cut with a pair of scissors"), Lean wasn't contributing only to the reductive requisites of the craft. In the heyday of the British quota quickie, when theaters had to field a proportion of British film fare far exceeding what the industry could decently assemble, Lean was hired to stretch and pad thin narrative material into feature-length program-fillers. In his hands, films would fatten through the ingenious plundering of stock footage, the artfully prolonged closeup, or the now-you-see-it-now-you-don't recycling of identical shots.

Here, in the unexpected ingenuities of expansionist editing, we might sense the first stirrings of Lean the epicmaker. "The hell with quickfire cutting and helter-skelter montage," he might have meditated. "May not the camera as profitably *linger* as leap about?"

The two warring sides of Lean the artist—the reductive and the accretive—are in full cry in his first directing assignment, *In Which We Serve*. Two of the sequences Lean is known to have masterminded, without the Master apparently minding, are the dive-bombing of the ship and Celia Johnson's Christmas dinner speech about the life of a sailor's wife. The first sequence is an example of the newsreelist's art transferred to feature film: a rat-a-rat montage of action and reaction, melee and mayhem, kaleidoscopically evoked. But in the second, linear Lean takes over to daring effect. He holds the camera on Johnson's face throughout the long speech without a single cutaway to the listeners, profoundly intensifying the emotional effect. Already in Lean's priorities the unblinking camera is favored for scenes of human interaction, while montage is ghettoed off for action scenes.

Startlingly early in his directing career, furthermore, Lean was flirting with the ambitious wonders of the 70mm lens. In *Great Expectations* he and art director John Bryan used 70mm and 50mm lenses in addition to the more normal 35mm; they even designed the sets to compensate for 70mm's shortened perspective by making them slope away from the camera. The strategy behind the use of different lenses is ingeniously illustrated in the depiction of Miss Havisham's house. When seen through the boy Pip's eyes, the sets look vast and cavernous (shot with a 24mm lens); but when seen through the older Pip's eyes, they seem small and enclosed (75mm lens).

It's the high definition and vivid foregrounding of 70mm that give Lean's Dickens films their immediacy—those luminous closeups that swirl across the screen with the vastness and detail of a natural landscape. When a journalist questioned Lean as to whether the average filmgoer would actually notice he was using a 70mm lens, Lean snapped quickly back, "Well, they don't notice the fourteen coats of paint on a Rolls-Royce, but they're still there."

Lean detractors will argue that cinematic Rolls-Royces are exactly what the director has increasingly devoted himself to creating. Vast, sleek, cushioned, and purring, his *Kwai*-and-after epics are designed to make ordinary feature films look like beat-up Chevvies. To filmgoers who couldn't give a damn about paintwork or upholstery, and just want to be driven wittily or dramatically from point A to point B, the late Lean style sometimes seems like so much inflated snobbism. Whereas the 70mm lens is used for precise dramatic purposes in *Great Expectations*, it's merely used for all-purpose five-star spectacle in *Kwai* or *Lawrence*. Whereas the sophisticated soundtrack in Lean's 1952 *The Sound Barrier* was used to evoke the experience of mach-1 flying, in *Zhivago* or *Ryan's Daughter* the sophisticated sound is just used to blandish us with wrap-around Muzak. Whereas the star casts of *Oliver Twist* or *Great Expectations* were handpicked to do justice to Dickens's exotics and grotesques, the star casts of the Lean blockbusters have less to do with the perfect or even plausible matching of actor to role (Guinness as an Arab prince?

Robert Mitchum as a tongue-tied Irish teacher? Omar Sharif as a struggling Russian poet-doctor?) than with shoring up the boxoffice with a roll call of thespian glamour.

To understand Lean, you have to understand the principles of detonation in the British artistic temperament, a process unlike any other on earth. When frustrated British reticence reaches fission point, it turns straight into holocaust grandiloquence: the paintings of Francis Bacon, the films of Michael Powell, the magic moments in Olivier's acting.

It's after *Summertime* that Lean became, spectacularly, his own master. It's as if the repressed British artist has sensed release at the call of fifties blockbusterism, just as in *Summertime* skittering Hepburn sloughs spinsterhood at the mating call of the Brazzi. There is no holding him as his screens get wider, his stories get longer, and we enter the strange new obsessive world of Lean elephantiasis. Here it can be argued that Lean's late luxuriant epics are more interesting, for all their fatuities, than his "perfect" apprentice work—as the products of individual preference are always more interesting than the execution (however flawless) of received rules (however golden).

Lean's epics have been known to cast a spell on impressionable and by no means negligible movie minds. No sooner did Luchino Visconti, for example, emerge in a guilty but rapturous glow from his first viewing of *Doctor Zhivago* than he said to his companion. "Let's see it round again. But don't tell anyone!" To hungry filmgoers who hold out their senses to the cinema saying. "Please, sir, can I have some more," Lean dishes out every ingredient we secretly want to guzzle. The all-star cast; the engulfing screen; the epic landscapes; the retina-whopping colors: the lush music; the wall-to-wall (and floor-to-ceiling) sound; the action- and passion-packed story; the rolling narrative surge, like a soap opera writ large, lyrical, and extra-lathery.

The trouble with Lean, of course, is that he takes all this so seriously. Instead of just giving us lavish potboilers, he pretends they're *magna opera. Gone with the Wind* and *Duel in the Sun* we can relish for their pop-operatic hyperbole, but there isn't a hint of camp or purple bravura in Lean. Ten-ton literary classics are out diet, or earnest hymns to the heroic spirit in war, or the growing pains of Irish history rhymed with the growing pains of Irish womanhood in *Ryan's Daughter*. Anyone caught laughing at the films or their perfervid pathos must stay and see Mr. Lean after class.

In adapting *A Passage to India*, Lean was keen to insure that Forster's independent-minded women—the young Adela Quested (Judy Davis) and the older Mrs. Moore (Peggy Ashcroft)—didn't come over as "aggressive." Ironically, Lean's women, certainly in his early films and even (if more simplemindedly) in *Ryan's Daughter*, have often been the feistiest of independents:

Jean Simmons's spitfire Estella in *Great Expectations*, Hepburn yacking her way to late-blooming sexuality in *Summertime*, and, of course, Celia Johnson taking a gulp and throwing propriety to the winds in *Brief Encounter*.

For the male artist—especially the British male artist—depicting the growth of passion and independence in a woman is a challenging task. Lean, who made his boldest attempt at it in *Brief Encounter*, perhaps never got over the traumatic experience of that film's first preview: "A woman in the front started laughing at the first love scene. Pretty soon the laughter spread right through the cinema. . . . I fled, convinced that I had a total disaster."

There's a strange reticence, a kind of throttled emotionalism, in Lean's films that does indeed suggest a fear of feeling or of the ridicule attending vulnerability. Lean is often far more confident handling the absurdist agonies of the constipated British soul—Guinness's Colonel Nicholson in *Kwai*, O'Toole's pale, agonized Lawrence—than with plonking big uncorseted emotions down on the screen.

Yet so, in a way, was E. M. Forster—that miniaturist of the heart whose characters never quite trust their own emotions, even when they're most passionately gripped by them. Lean's challenge in *A Passage to India* was to marry his subtle gaucherie of feeling with an insight into the novel's tragic collision of human value systems and cosmic nihilism and to make the British movie about India "to which all others are trailers."

Old stone bridge, fluffed-up swans gliding on artificial lake, palms and orange trees, rioting ferns, flaming oleanders, trees I cannot name. Pink stone arches, long corridor leading to a lush rattan-furnished suite with indoor palm. No, not India—Hollywood. The Bel Air Hotel, where Sir David Lean, silver and seigneurial, welcomes me in. Glimpses of our conversation about *A Passage to India* follow.

Q:    *When did you first read* A Passage to India?
A:    You know, I cannot remember. It's a jolly hard book to read—it's tough. Have you been dipping in? (*Yes.*) I'll tell you a fascinating thing about it. Do you want me to go on and talk like this? (*Sure.*) I like a fairly strong narrative in a film and [E. M.] Forster—I don't think he's as concerned with narrative as a lot of people would claim. The trouble with making a film is that he keeps going off on the most wonderful sidetracks, and one is tempted to go down them with him. One writes pages of script and then thinks, "Well, wait a minute; I've gone off the story."

And then you have to cut, because it's a huge book. It was terribly difficult, because he's got a narrative there but it's awfully hard to find it. I used to sit myself down and think, "Now what is this section really about?" Now the end section—that's a fine kettle of fish. New characters popping up, a dying Rajah, and so on. Aziz letting his instruments rust.

Q: *Obviously you had to collapse incidents, and a portion of the film totally invented by you, which does not derive from Forster, is the scene where Adela Quested (Judy Davis) goes cycling in the country and discovers an overgrown temple encrusted with marvelous erotic carvings of couples . . . well, coupling.*
A: That's totally mine, yes. You see the reason why?

Q: *It depicts the sexual stirrings and awakening of desire within Adela.*
A: Correct. In the book and in the play particularly, I must tell you, Miss Quested was an absolute "stick," and I thought she was quite uninteresting. And when the idea is presented that Aziz had attempted whatever he attempted, in the caves, I thought, "What?" It didn't work. And I wanted to set it up so that you could argue afterwards, "Did he? Didn't he?" In the book and in the play Miss Quested was not a believable character on the whole, as far as her sexuality was concerned. I thought that I had to find a way that fills her out a little more, to let you see that she is beginning to awaken sexually . . . because India can do this, you know. There are two lots of people that go to India: Some get off the plane and want to get the next plane out; others want to stay for six months—and she obviously is one who wanted to stay for six months, and I wanted to catch a bit of that.

Q: *Was the temple real or a construction?*
A: A couple of the long shots of the temple through trees are real; the rest is constructed in little bits and pieces cut together. It was all shot in different places, and I didn't know until I cut it if it would work—I went out on a limb. It does work, doesn't it?

Q: *Indeed it does.*
A: Good. I meant it to be sort of sexually frightening—you know, her feelings, the roaring, and, my God, the monkeys going after her.

Q: *Does this scene marry with a line—not in the book—at the trial in which she states that she did not love Ronny her fiancé?*
A: "Seeing Chandrapore so far away, I realized I didn't love him." That's me. I was trying to make her go, as it were, almost into the past so that she's removed from the town, Ronny, just that. You know, it happens to people when they go down to the Mediterranean on holiday—Swedes, Finns, English people—come down to Spain and behave as they wouldn't normally. It's that sort of thing. And so the idea is that it's a sort of walk into old places, old mountains with that old ancient animal climbing up them.

Q:    *The mountain is fantastic.*

A:    It's good, isn't it? It works. Because we went all over the place looking for that, and I found it. Nobody knew about it, because it's such a huge country. And it's about an hour out of Bangalore.

Q:    *There's a remarkable lack of music in the film. All the drama is in the voices and images. I also noticed that you were cutting on particular words. For instance, someone would say, "Tomorrow we are in Ranjipur," and we cut to Ranjipur. Is this a purposeful technique you were using—opposed to dissolves?*

A:    I rather like the technique. I haven't got many dissolves. In fact I've only got one fade-in, fade-out, which goes from the crocodile to the garden party. And there was a good reason for that, because I suddenly realized that to cut from the crocodile eating a body to "tea for two" . . . well, wiseacres would find that very funny. So I faded out and faded in, to separate them.

Q:    *In the trial scene you intercut between the earlier Judy Davis cave scene and the trial to illustrate her state of mind.*

A:    Yes. When you have the court scene she says, "I lit a match," and I cut back to her in the cave looking out, and Aziz appears at the entrance of the cave; then I cut back to her in court looking at the cave. And you hear the voice, and it follows you. I was awfully pleased with that, and I thought it worked.

It's quite interesting the way you can cut and jump around in time in movies—I don't think it's been done too often—and there's enormous scope for it, as long as it's crystal clear so that you don't lose your audience and have them thinking, "What the hell is that?"

Q:    *Again in Forster, at the garden party (or the "bridge party," as he calls it) all the Indian men were dressed in European fashion, and it was very uncomfortable. But in the film it looks so nice that it doesn't look bad or uncomfortable—and the dialogue about "Why aren't we treating our guests. . . . "*

A:    Well, I thought it was bad enough to have the English characters all seated up on a raised part and the Indians standing below, just being totally ignored, looking up. I think Forster went a little bit overboard. I must tell you that one or two people objected that in the trial, which I practically rewrote and made a big scene of it, I put Mrs. Moore's death in the middle because I wanted Mrs. Moore to hang over the trial. I think it works.

One of the biggest scenes in the book is that at the trial all the English take their seats and move up on the platform until they're told by Das, the trial judge, to move down. I believe it would look really stupid if you're going to have a trial at which Aziz and eventually the girl are up against the English—they've got to be worthy opponents. And people moving their chairs up and down would be wrong. I'm glad I made that change, though many people said that Forster had them move up and down. . . . I know he did that but I refrained from doing it very purposefully in the same way I didn't "guy" the Indians with spats and awkward collars—I think it's a bit corny.

Q:    *How did you attempt to duplicate the mystical sound, the "ou- boum" Forster describes as a property of the caves? It was almost mocking—the eternal mocking the temporal.*
A:    You know, it's very interesting, but booms were attacked like mad at the time by D. H. Lawrence, for instance. . . . But Forster said, and I think it's rather good, that the boom was a trick which he would have attempted nowhere else but in India. And it was, of course, a very worrying thing for me because if "BOOM" doesn't work, the whole cave incident doesn't work, and you've got everything falling in on you.

Q:    *Was Forster right about the British in India?*
A:    Forster, oh dear, oh dear. I think he hated the English out there. And he was queer, and you can imagine how they must have disapproved of that— this damned Englishman working for a Maharajah. The dislike was mutual, but I've toned down a lot of that. It's all very well to criticize the English but just take a look at New Delhi, look at the railway system, look at the postal system—which works. We've left them all sorts of bad things, I suppose, but they also got some very good things.

Q:    *Do you feel that Forster's portrayal of the British woman in India was a fair one?*
A:    I think that was more or less fair. In fact, I've made it rather worse, if anything. I've taken some of the worst stuff and put it on to the women, on to Mrs. Turton, the Collector's wife, rather than the men, because I don't think the men were all a lot of fools. It's awfully easy to sit back and say they were a lot of clowns. They weren't. But you can still meet these women in India today. Mrs. Turton would be retired and find herself having had twelve servants suddenly lucky that she has one. She doesn't know what hit her. It's rather sad, really. Because they lived a tremendous life out there—created their own towns.

Q:    *But the British of today have integrated themselves more fully into Indian life.*
A:    Well, I'm quite a good example. I married one. I was married to her for several years.

Q:    *You can't get closer than that, I guess.*
A:    Guess not.

Q:   *Now about the play* A Passage to India, *by Santha Rama Rau . . .*

A:   I'll tell you a funny thing about that. I saw the play about twenty-five years ago, and it was a terrible thing because Norman Wooland—he was in Larry Olivier's *Hamlet*—played Fielding. He was awfully good, and I could not get his face out of my head. Whenever I thought of Fielding, I saw Norman Wooland up there superimposed over everything. The same thing happened with Zia Mohyeddin, who was very good as Aziz. (I gave him a small part as the guide to Peter O'Toole in *Lawrence*.) He was too old for Aziz now, and I believe it broke his heart because he wanted to be in it. And I just couldn't get his face out of my head. Now, I'm glad to say, they've been supplanted, but they're hovering there. . . .

Q:   *Why do you keep working with Sir Alec Guinness?*

A:   Well, Alec started his film career with me on *Great Expectations*, then he did *Oliver Twist, Bridge on the River Kwai*, and *Lawrence of Arabia*. It was rather a good working partnership. I like Alec. And I think he has the most difficult role in this film. It required a tremendously good character actor to bring it off, I think.

Q:   *Why is it the most difficult role in the film?*

A:   You see, Godbole is everything. He's sort of first cousin to Mrs. Moore, he's got a sort of extrasensory perception—at least I gave him that; he's part mumbo-jumbo, part highly intelligent, cynical, part funny. It's a real bag of tricks to contain in one character.

Q:   *How do you prepare your films? Do you storyboard, do you do step-outs?*

A:   I nearly always write the shooting script and imagine seeing it as a finished film on screen. I think that this might be good in a long shot, that in a close-up, that in a panning shot. And I try to write down the pictures that I see on an imaginary screen. I'm a picture chap, I like pictures, and when I go to the movies I go to see pictures. I think dialogue is nearly always secondary in a movie. It's awfully hard when you look back over the really great movies that you see in your life to remember a line of dialogue. You will not forget pictures.

Q:   *What films do you like?*

A:   People ask me this, and so I'm wheeling out old answers. I remember when I first went to the movies, they hit me right in the eyeball. I'll never forget seeing *Four Horsemen of the Apocalypse*. It had a wonderful sweep to it. And I saw it again only a few years ago, here in Los Angeles at FILMEX. A new print and a forty-piece orchestra. Absolutely stunning, I thought. And I also like stars. It became a sort of thing to laugh at Valentino, Errol Flynn. God's sake, they were both terrific. Go and see *Dawn Patrol*, go and see *Robin Hood*—Fairbanks and Flynn. Wonderful! Wonderful people to watch!

I suppose it was those early moviemakers mostly I remember as a boy . . . getting out of the suburbs of London and into a really magic house . . . looking at that beam of light coming through the smoke. There were things on the screen that you thought you'd never ever see in real life, and I've been lucky enough to see a lot of them. I'll never forget seeing King Vidor's *The Big Parade* with John Gilbert and Renee Adore saying "Goodbye" with the trucks going up to the "Front," and her left alone and everything moving against her. I've used it several times. I love that business with a single figure against moving people. . . . And then much later the shock of seeing *Citizen Kane* and the way Orson turned everything upside down. Wonderful, that dance he had with the girls in the newspaper office. Terrific! Hard to do that sort of thing.

Q:    *Have you seen* Gandhi?
A:    I have and I haven't. In India I saw a pirated tape which was a good half hour short, and it was an appalling quality. So I can't really say that I've seen *Gandhi*.

Q:    *Why is there this sudden interest in India? Spielberg had a short sequence in* Close Encounters, *plus* Indiana Jones, Gandhi, *two TV mini-series,* The Far Pavilions *and* Jewel in the Crown. *And now Judith de Paul has just completed* Mountbatten *in India.*
A:    People asked me that in India. They sort of approached me with a know-ing smile. (Lean in imitation of Indian speech). "I suppose you are cashing eeen on the present trend," or something like that. I think it's coincidence. I know we weren't trying to cash in on anything. . . . Kubrick did *2001*, and since then we've had a rash of space operas. Somebody will do a hit film about New Zealanders and everybody will rush off to New Zealand! That's movies.

# Return Passage

## GRAHAM FULLER AND NICHOLAS KENT / 1985

DAVID LEAN'S FILMS are not everyone's cup of tea. From *Lawrence of Arabia* (1962) onwards they have earned the most sarcastic similes that the critics, especially those in America, have been able to dream up. No matter that *Lawrence, Doctor Zhivago*, and *Ryan's Daughter* have each been popular successes with the public and claimed many awards, they have been dismissed by the press as "hollow" and "middlebrow." Against this backdrop of disapproval, therefore, Lean's re-emergence with *A Passage to India*—at the age of seventy-six and after fourteen years away from filmmaking—must be regarded as all the more remarkable.

If the emotional flavour of his films and their grandeur of conception has provided the basis for debate about Lean's work, their technical excellence has never been in dispute. The creator of *Brief Encounter, The Bridge on the River Kwai, Lawrence*, and *Zhivago* is a master craftsman whose creative flair has less to do with big budgets and exotic locations than the impeccable credentials of his apprenticeship in the British film industry in the thirties. It was there, after all, that Lean learned his editing skills and studied the techniques of framing, composition and movement that became vital to his own highly visual movies.

Lean was a Quaker's son, born in Croydon, Surrey, on 25 March 1908, and forbidden to go to the cinema. At school in Reading, however, he escaped to matinees and became entranced by silent films. He followed his father into accountancy, but the film industry beckoned, and in 1927 he got work as a tea boy at Gainsborough studios. He ran the gamut of studio jobs—runner, clapper/loader, focus-puller, wardrobe "mistress"—and eventually edged his way into the cutting rooms.

From *Stills* (March 1985).

In 1930 Lean became assistant editor at British Movietone News and, sharpening his talent, was soon the editor there. At Paramount-British from 1934, he cut "quota quickies" and was given a major run out on *Escape Me Never*. By the end of the decade he was Britain's highest paid film editor, the man entrusted with such prestige projects as *Pygmalion*, *Major Barbara*, and *49th Parallel*. In 1942 Noel Coward hired him as co-director on the wartime naval story *In Which We Serve*, and Lean directed most of it. They collaborated together on three more films, of which *Brief Encounter* became a classic of suburban English love.

Lean followed with his unsurpassed adaptations from Dickens, produced at Cineguild (the company he had founded with Ronald Neame and Anthony Havelock-Allan), then three films starring his then wife Ann Todd. The last of these, *The Sound Barrier*, was made for Alexander Korda's London Films after Cineguild had disbanded. Next came a Lancashire comedy, British Lion's *Hobson's Choice*, and the gloriously realized Venice romance of *Summer Madness* for Korda. Lean now embarked on his major epics—*Kwai* and *Lawrence* for Sam Spiegel, *Zhivago* for Carlo Ponti, and *Ryan's Daughter* for Allan.

The failure to get *The Bounty* off the ground in the early eighties was a personal tragedy for Lean, but a new horizon—India—summoned him from the wreckage of that project.

Q:    *Your previous film,* Ryan's Daughter, *came out in 1970. After such a long absence, how was it to get back into making films again? Did you approach it with trepidation?*
A:    Not more than usual. But it's always difficult. Always you have terrible doubts suddenly sweep over you. We filmmakers are always engaged on prototypes—it isn't as if we're making a car and we're going to build four hundred models. We just make a film and that's it—now off onto something else. As you know, I've done films in all sorts of styles—I remember Noel Coward used to say to me, "Always come out of another hole."

Q:    *What was it then that particularly impressed you about E. M. Forster's novel* A Passage to India *as being fitting for treatment on the screen? Was it the narrative?*
A:    It has four or five wonderful characters, but Forster doesn't—as you have to do in a film—have a well-defined thread going through it. One of the difficulties was not to be tempted by side-tracks. He is a wonderful side-tracker. His sidetracks are most entertaining reading, but I don't think they're necessarily film material.

Q:    *It would have been intriguing to know what Forster would have thought of the film because he is said to have had an extraordinary distrust of cinema.*

A:    When you say a distrust of cinema, I think he didn't trust it entirely in this particular case because he was frightened that if a movie was made it would come down on the side of the English or on the side of the Indians. And he said he wouldn't sell it while he was alive for that reason. In fact, I think Forster came down hard against the English and very much for the Indians. I tried to balance it a bit more.

Q:    *When you came to shoot* A Passage to India *was everything pre-planned? Do you have all the scenes set up in your mind when you start filming, and can you adjust if necessary?*
A:    It's not a question of "can," you've bloody got to. I sit down and I work on the script and I try to write it down as I imagine it's going to be up there on the screen. When I've got a negative in the form of a script and dialogue, I've then got to try to match it with the actors, the sets, the camerawork, and all the rest of it. And sometimes it's very difficult. Maybe an actor can't do exactly what you thought, so you've got to re-think it a bit. But I do try to get it all down. There are always things which you thought were going to be perfectly easy and something comes up that absolutely throws it.

At the very beginning of *A Passage to India* it was tough—that parade with the Viceroy arriving in India. I thought we were going to do it all at the Gateway of India in Bombay, but we arrived there and found that since my time they'd built a huge harbour and public gardens. So that was a bit devastating. You can't stage a parade there, and if you could you wouldn't be able to keep the crowds away. There was no big amount of troops in Bombay. They were in Delhi. So we did a matte shot. We photographed the Gateway of India in Bombay; we did the shots of the Viceroy coming through it with the carpet in Bombay; the sea is taken somewhere near Bombay; the arch is Bombay; all the crowds are in Delhi. It's all combined in a trick shot—not because I wanted to do a trick shot but because one couldn't get it otherwise, and I was determined to use the Gateway of India. It was a heck of a job.

Q:    *Was it more arduous shooting in India compared with location work on your other films?*
A:    No, not really. We were in Bangalore, 3,000 feet up, lovely weather, beautiful place, lovely trees. I enjoyed it. We were working in a maharaja's palace. So it was very contained on the whole. Much more than *Lawrence*. *Lawrence*, for God's sake, I mean we started off in Jordan, then transferred to Spain, then had to go for the final scenes to Morocco.

*Zhivago* was all in Spain except for two weeks in Finland, but was terribly difficult you see. Sure enough, if you're writing a storm or you're writing a snow scene, everyone will say, "From November on it's going to snow like mad." or "There's going to be a very rough sea." And November will come and end and they say, "Well, it's the first time we've ever known it calm in November," or "It's the first time we've never had snow in November." That happened to me on *Zhivago*. We had that house out on the plain, and we had artificial snow on the domes and the roof. And there it remained. They said, "Look, at the end of November the snow will begin." We waited till the end of November. No snow. December, January, and February and there it was, sitting out in this huge plain with yellow stubble. And the first week of March we got a telephone call: "It's snowing!" We dashed out there and we shot all that snow stuff in three days, praying that it wasn't going to melt too fast. That sort of thing happens.

A thing like a storm, the *Ryan's Daughter* storm, was shot in three different storms. Very intricate job of cutting. A chap called Roy Stephens who was my assistant director did the second unit on that, and I'd say, "Get a close up of Leo McKern with water *pouring* over him." And that was actually a "tip" tank full of water emptied over him, and that would be intercut with another shot of him standing there with the waves in the background. It's a cutting job and it takes a long time.

Q:   *Did the light cause any particular problems in India?*

A:   It was the same as on Lawrence. You have to use quite a lot of light on exteriors because at midday the sun's almost overhead, so there's no light on the eyes. There's the top of your head, the end of your nose and your chin. But it's terribly contrasty, you know, black and white. And you want to see the eyes of an actor on most occasions, so in that tropical sun you have to bang in artificial light to lighten up the shadows. We were out in the desert with Lawrence, away from anything, and we had to have a light that in those days was called a brute, a huge great thing. Now the lights have got much smaller thank goodness.

Q:   *Because of the wide pictorial scope of your films the initial visualization is obviously a major part of the process. When you were working on the script for* A Passage to India *did you draw sketches or storyboard it?*

A:   I can't draw.

Q:   *So how do you communicate what you want to achieve to your crew?*

A:   Well, I tell them first of all to read, and then we have a talk. And if there's something very complicated or there are any disagreements, I sit down with a sketch artist and say, "Let's draw that page." And he'll say, "How did you mean that? Did you mean it like that?" And I'll say, "No, I saw it from a low angle like that." And he does it, and that's it. But I think storyboards are very clever—

I saw an interview with Spielberg and he said that he liked them because people could make various interpretations of the written word, but there was no argument over a storyboard. And I think that has great use because you'll give a scene to four people—nobody really reads carefully—and you find each of these people will come in with a different version of what it's going to look like.

It's a personality thing.

Q:  *Do you suggest to a cinematographer that he zooms or pans or tracks, or do you give him an impression of what you want and then leave it up to him? In what sort of circumstances do you choose to have a static or a moving camera?*

A:  I tell the cameraman *exactly* what I want. I choose the lens. In fact, I get a viewfinder, fiddle around with the various lenses on it, and then I say, "Here." They'll drop a chalk from the bottom of the viewfinder onto the floor and make a cross there, and then measure the height I am from the ground and then put the camera at the same height and in exactly the same position.

I've had cameramen who've seen me worry and scratch my head and they'll say, "I don't know what you're worrying about. This is the best angle, surely?" And I'll say, "Look, you're choosing the best view of the situation. And I don't think it's very interesting." There's something about the movement of a camera, whether it's panning or tracking, and I'm not mad about that sort of thing. It can be terribly show-offy. But there are occasions when it can be almost sensual, and sometimes it can be highly dramatic.

Whenever you talk of a track, I think of Lewis Milestone in *All Quiet on the Western Front*. When that attack starts and they start coming over the top, he tracks along the whole length of that trench. It's a fantastic effect. You could ask him why he does that, and I suppose he would answer that he thought it would raise the dramatic intensity rather than having a still camera showing men get up over the top and running. It's a sort of point of view. It's a cinematic idea.

Q:  *You often use a point-of-view camera, literally, for people moving down a road. For example, it's used very effectively at the beginning of* Lawrence of Arabia *with Lawrence traveling on the motorbike.*

A:  That's right. That's a good example. For instance, I could just show a man on a motorbike going down a road. I try to put the audience in the position of the man on the motorbike so that when two bicycles appear you think, "Christ, look out!" like him. I think that's more interesting than just having it in a long shot. I'd rather do it in a series of quick cuts, which give the audience the impression of being in on the crash.

Q: *Would you say that in your films as a whole you're seeing it from the hero's point of view?*
A: Not necessarily the hero's point of view. It's very useful every now and again to put the audience in the position of one of the characters. And I do it a lot. I do it a bit at the beginning of *A Passage to India*. I was trying to give the impression of these two women, one old, one young, seeing India for the first time. It was rather a sort of copy of when I first landed in Bombay years and years ago. Tremendous noise, tremendous bustle. I slightly exaggerated it on the screen. When they were walking by the side of the dock, I put in people crossing in front everywhere and made the noise rather bigger than it would be. The sudden pandemonium as you arrive in India—it's something quite different from the noise in Paddington Station.

Q: *How do you go about achieving a sense of rhythm in your films? It's been said of your work that it's largely attributable to the editing.*
A: It's a combination. It's movement combined with cuts. I'll say to actors, "Go over to the door. Open it. Look back. Go out. Try to get round it." It's rather like a dance, and it's pleasing. And in the same way that the moment you cut to the close-up, as they turn or whatever it is, and then they turn and look and you cut to that—there's a kind of flow in that. I mean, a movie is a flow of pictures isn't it?

Q: *Sometimes, though, a jump cut can be very strikingly effective. You use them yourself. For example, in* Lawrence of Arabia *you cut from the flame of a match being lit in England to the desert in Arabia, and in* Ryan's Daughter *you cut from the sun going down to another match being lit indoors.*
A: That's fine if you want to be strikingly effective, maybe it should all be staccato. You have to choose your technique—you may want the thing to have a sort of sensual flow to it, which I find very interesting. It's like music in a way. I often think of scenes in musical terms. They build up to a climax, then hover for a moment, and then . . . bok! I'll try to do that visually sometimes. Very akin to music, I think, the flow of pictures. The intensity of a scene going up to a peak, relaxing, and then bang!

Q: *Are your films ever cut in the camera—do you know where you're going to cut when you're actually shooting a scene?*
A: No. Lots of people say that sort of thing. I don't believe anybody cuts in the camera. I know quite a bit about cutting and I make a guess at it, but I'll always cover myself. I've been caught once or twice when my guess was wrong, and I don't believe there's *anybody* who can cut a picture in a camera. You can make an approximation. I mean I shoot very little film compared with a lot

of directors because I make a fairly good go at it. I could never be absolutely
right. It's hard enough when you've actually got all the film there. I'll cut and
re-cut perhaps three or four times before I'm happy with a scene.

Q:  *Is there a scene or a sequence in* A Passage to India *where the editing, the "flow
of pictures" particularly came off for you?*
A:  Well, there are a few, yes. I think the one that works best of all is the trial
scene. I think Judy Davis was absolutely marvellous in it. That business—
"Now, Miss Quested, cast your mind back," and she looks down and sees his
hand clasp hers earlier in the film, and you come back to her in the box thinking of it. It's that cutting forward that interests me, so you cut back to her.
"Miss Quested," you hear. "Miss Quested"—"Yes?"—and off you go.

And then she's back in the cave again, and there are a couple of cuts I'm awfully pleased with there, because it was quite a risk. She says, "I lit a match"—
you cut to the match being struck in the cave. Then he appears in the cave and
you are in the cave with her, and she's looking at him in the entrance. Then
you cut back to him in the entrance of the cave; then you cut back to her as
if looking at him from the dock, in the witness box—and back to him again.
And it all works. I thought it was an interesting piece of pictorial juxtaposition
between the past and the present. I'm awfully pleased with the way you can
cut around in time. And you know that certain things work and certain things
don't!

Q:  *James Fox, who plays Fielding in* A Passage to India, *has said that you are
more interested in the technical external aspects of acting than the spontaneous internal aspects.*
A:  Well, it's a lot of nonsense really. I've done my internal work in the script.
I'm surprised James doesn't realize that. The whole motivation of characters
is worked out in the script. It's no use saying, "He's keeping a brave exterior
but underneath his heart's going like mad and he's thinking of his mother
or whatever it is . . . " That's the whole thing with this Method school of acting isn't it? They've got to work out a story for themselves. I always say to
actors, "Film acting is *thinking.* It's not pulling faces." A good actor, I'm sure,
will be thinking a specific thought all the time. He will have worked out for
himself when he's studying the scene what he's thinking about. Whether he's
thinking about himself or whether he's thinking about what the person has
just said. I'd have a fine old time with every actor discussing what his inner
thoughts are on the set, wouldn't I?

I very rarely rehearse with actors before shooting, particularly on a script like
*A Passage to India.* There are very few set scenes. They'll be on a train one moment, leaving a boat the next. It's not a sit-down-and-talk, it's a flow of scenes.

Q:    *How did you find it working with Victor Bannerjee? Did you notice a particularly distinctive style of acting he had from his experience in the Indian cinema, and was there any kind of cultural gap you had to cross stylistically in terms of working with him as an actor?*

A:    I hadn't seen him on the screen before. I'd just talked to him. Two things: in Indian films on the whole, Indians, as far as our taste is concerned, overact grossly. They roll their eyes, shout, and certainly wave their arms about. If an actor is nervous, as somebody like Victor obviously was at the beginning of this picture, I'd tell him please to keep very still, just think, just look at the man. Don't look over there. Don't look over there. Just keep still. And after a bit, look down and move a finger.

He'll start to lose his nerve because he'll think that he's doing nothing, that he's sitting there like a dummy and nothing is coming through. In fact, the opposite is the case. All the big stars know all about keeping still. I saw Jack Nicholson the other day in *Chinatown*. Marvellous performance—and most of the time he was absolutely still. It takes a terrific nerve to do it.

I remember I cut *Pygmalion* with Leslie Howard, and sometimes I'd watch him and I'd think, "Well, you've gone too far. You're doing absolutely nothing." See him on the screen, see that same shot in close-up—it's riveting, because he's concentrating and thinking. It's like a dynamo that's run up just before the take. It goes up and up and up until it's got to quite a pitch. And then "Action!"—and then it'll come out. And I think people don't quite realize that.

Q:    *You and Victor Bannerjee had some disagreements over the accent Dr. Aziz was going to use. Can you elaborate on that?*

A:    That story's never been properly told. I wanted Victor to speak as most Indians do. The dialogue was written to be said in that way. Now Victor thought that I was trying to guy the Indians. I wasn't. I wanted Dr. Aziz to start as kind of naive—the more goofy he was in the beginning, the greater the transformation would be after the trial. In my opinion Victor missed that for the wrong reasons. I was so cross I seriously thought of post-synching him and putting in another voice. I don't blame Victor. I do understand. We were, as it were, an army of occupation.

Q:    *Did your experience of going to see films when you were young affect the way you later presented your own films to an audience?*

A:    In the old days when you went to see a film, the lights would go out and, if it was really good, it would get hold of me and the audience would disappear and my vision would narrow down so it was just me and the screen.

One aspect of silent films was that they were black and white—that removed it one stage from reality—and, two, you didn't hear characters speaking.

You just had subtitles and so you imagined things. And, three, the wonderful thing was that there was a live orchestra there. And you, the audience, were *involved* in what was happening on the screen, and you were *contributing* to it. And when talkies came, everything was completely frozen. The stories were spelt out, and the audience were left just as spectators and not as participants.

A few years ago I saw a new print of Rex Ingram's *The Four Horsemen of the Apocalypse* at Filmex run at the right speed with a forty-piece orchestra. Marvellous! Now there were all sorts of things in it which were rather overdone in present terms, but in emotion, in sweep, it left us standing. You were really participating. I *love* that.

I try to encourage the audience to participate in films. Tricky business because it's a bit risky. If I can get a scene in the cinema that is quiet enough and subtle enough that the audience are coming forward to watch every movement, I'm getting back a little bit to the silent days when they were doing just that. I know some people call it old-fashioned now. I don't think it is.

Q:   *When you're writing a script, you have a very clear idea of what you want to see on the screen. How clear is your idea of what you want to hear?*
A:   Well, we were so short of money on *A Passage to India* that I didn't write any music into the script (except in the last bit with the Himalayas). I regret that. Of course, I'm terribly conscious of the sound track, which is almost as important as the pictures. For instance, when Omar Sharif comes out of the desert in *Lawrence*, the sound editor Winston Ryder put in the pad, pad, pad of the camel's feet. It wasn't a real sound, but it added immeasurably to the silence of the desert, the size of it all.

In *Passage* I think we got rather a good sound track with the visit of the girl to the temple. We got monkey noises and Win said, "I think they're too high pitched. They're not menacing enough." So we re-recorded all the monkey noises at about a quarter speed so that they all went down in tone. We took a lot of care over that and it worked. And then the music comes in and combines with the rustle of leaves and the bicycle noise. It creates an atmosphere to counterpoint the action.

Q:   *Steven Spielberg and his colleagues obviously have great respect for your work. What are your views of the "movie brat" generation and their work?*
A:   Spielberg is an exception. He is an extraordinary chap. The first time you saw *Duel* you knew he was a *director*. And I thought some of *Jaws*—which let's face it is not the greatest literature—really kept you on the edge of your seat. I jumped like mad at all sorts of moments. I think he's especially talented, but on the whole I don't think some of the others are terribly good storytellers.

They're very good *episodic* directors; their films are like a series of episodes. And I don't think they're very great at character. They go in for black and white heroes and villains. Their style is a bit show-off, and I think the best films aren't. In the old days I wasn't conscious of the director saying, "Now we're going to do this. Now we're going to give you a shock."

Q:    *In the past, you've had quite a rough ride from some of the critics, particularly in America and particularly with* Ryan's Daughter. *Their opinions obviously matter to you. Why is that?*
A:    The critics are the only people who, as it were, give an appreciation of a film when it's finished. Obviously, you have no contact with the public whatever, and you can't go round and stand outside the theatre and say, "What do you think?" And also, the critics are the ones who put it into *print*. If you pick up a critic who seems to be writing in measured terms, you think, "Now wait a minute, I wonder if he's right?" There it is written down—*The Times* says so, the *Daily Telegraph* says so, the *Daily Mail* says so, all shades of opinion—and it *must* be true.

I remember in America we had a dinner after the premiere of *Zhivago* and the papers started coming in and everybody was reading these terrible reviews. *Newsweek*, I remember, was the first notice that came out, and one of the expressions was "Cheapjack sets and pallid photography." But it won the Oscars for sets and for photography, and it wasn't cheap at all. And as the dinner ended, it was like some awful funeral. People kept coming up to me and saying, "Well David, well Mr. Lean, I enjoyed it. I'm sure business will pick up." But it took four weeks because of the reviews for business to pick up.

Q:    *Did you go into any cinemas anonymously in America to try and gauge an audience's response to* A Passage to India?
A:    Well, yes, and it's very odd. As the film progresses, the audience gets quieter and quieter, and when one gets to the trial, it's almost as if they're all in aspic, it's almost as if they've been mesmerized.

And when the film finishes there's a dead silence, no applause, the titles come up, they sit there, and then they start to get up and go. And you just don't know what they're thinking.

# David Lean: Reviving the Image

## JEAN-LUC SABLON/1989

IN THE DOCKS OF LIMEHOUSE, where the ghosts of Francis Carco and the memories of Mac Orlan are still prowling, David Lean, eighty-two, has arranged a little paradise: an English lawn (gardening is one of his hobbies) where countless holiday souvenirs are displayed. This man, who considers his passions to be cinema and hotels, has decided to settle down here, across the Thames, where his grandparents, the Tangyes, have tested their industrial inventions on the boats of the Great Eastern.

David Lean is working. He is finishing off counting the accessories of *Nostromo*, the scenario he has just completed together with Robert Bolt, based on a novel by Joseph Conrad. Following the failure to shoot the *Mutiny on the Bounty*—"this was the masterpiece of Bolt's"—he has dived into this new adventure: *Nostromo* is expected to begin shooting this winter in Mexico.

One says he is biting—in fact he is joyful. One knows him as a perfectionist—in fact he is. David Lean does not particularly like discussing his memories, he gets lost in the dates with indifference. However, his childhood is very present. So how does the son of an accountant come to dream and direct *Lawrence of Arabia*, *Doctor Zhivago*, and *Ryan's Daughter*? With a smile, David Lean agrees to explain.

Q: *When you were young, did you know about T. E. Lawrence?*
A: I don't remember it was so long ago. But as far as I can remember, Lawrence was a hero. I do remember the pictures of him in the newspapers during the Conference of Versailles. I was eleven years old . . .

Q: *This was the time of the first big film stars. Pola Negri was huge.*

---

Originally published in *La Revue de Cinema* (June 1989). Translated from the French by Antoine Larpin with Steven Organ.

A:  She was beautiful. Yes. Someone said that she was in love with Rudolph Valentino, who I also admired.

Q:  *Where did you come up with the idea for* Lawrence of Arabia*?*
A:  I had two ideas in mind—do not ask me which year it was. I had done *The Bridge on the River Kwai* for Sam Spiegel and Sam had asked me: "Do you have another idea, baby?" I said yes. My first idea was *Gandhi*, a film on which I had done a lot of work. I worked with two writers; one of them was Emeric Pressburger—who used to work with Michael Powell. So I travelled to India . . . and I met Nehru, you see. (Very nice, really. And I remember Miss Gandhi, who was very young.) Nehru was one of the most fascinating people I had ever met. The top of his face was that of a poet. And the bottom, very sensual. . . . One night we were having dinner when he told me: "Fresh mangos are coming up. Do you know how to cut a mango?" and I answered: "Uhh . . . ." and he showed me. He had this sort of kindness. He told me that Gandhi would always travel in premium class and that he would bring a goat, for the milk. An extra carriage was always necessary for Gandhi. Very frankly, he said, it cost them a fortune to keep Gandhi poor. Well, you must go back in the past, good Lord! Sam Spiegel came to India. He did not really like it.

Q:  *Why not?*
A:  You don't know Sam?

Q:  *No.*
A:  I liked him very much but he was a crook. Yet I had a lot of affection for him. He had a lot of charisma and he was a gambler. But Sam and India did not work together. There are two types of people, those who come to India and want to leave on the next plane and those who fall in love with it. Spiegel left immediately. So, I had two projects, and I told him the other was *Lawrence of Arabia*. (He had never heard of it. It is true, but at the time, no Americans knew who Lawrence was.) Finally, I wasn't able to get started on *Gandhi*, though I would return to the project much later. At that time I hoped that Alec Guinness could play Gandhi. So Sam convinced me to do *Lawrence* and I was happy with this decision. I like the film as it is. Have you seen this version?

Q:  *The revised?*
A:  It is not revised. We only added what Sam had cut off. The work they have done on the restoration in the U.S. is fantastic. For the sound we did not have any of the original materials—all of it had been thrown away. The tapes, the script, and the film were shot in 65mm, and 65mm is like 70mm film stock with the difference being that you keep 5mm on the positive to make some room for the stereo tracks. It is a 65mm negative, and we edit it on 70mm.

That's it. We don't blow up anything. There was one copy left that was acceptable. Nearly twenty-five minutes were missing. Obviously, I knew nothing about those edits. I knew about a cut of six minutes that I did—Sam had asked me to cut a little, for the TV—so I made some cuts at the beginning of the film, approximately six minutes. But I didn't know that Sam had retouched the rest, two weeks after the premiere. I also didn't know it was a success either. I knew that the film had obtained an Oscar, but I had been told that the film was only doing well in big cities.

Q:   *You had been duped, financially.*
A:   Yes. I didn't get a single penny for ten or fifteen years. Brief as it was.

Q:   *Robert Bolt says that Sam Spiegel wanted to add a role for a woman . . .*
A:   I don't remember. But obviously, I'm not surprised.

So, we only had this one copy, and the dialogue, the music, the sound effects were on another sound track, all of this was not on the track of this copy. It was very difficult to edit. The Americans have recorded all of this in digital sound, at the Goldwyn studios, and put it back on six tracks in Dolby. It is far better than before. The negative was torn over two meters, luckily along the perforations. The lab at the Goldwyn studios has done a fantastic job. They have cleaned everything up, fixed it up picture-by-picture and have printed a copy. I have seen their first copy and I asked: "Why is it so much better than in the past?" and they tell me it is because they worked on a very recent film stock, with a very thin grain. When you print this, they said, a transcript, a copy of a copy, it is better because it has better definition. It is wonderful. Colours, definition, everything. Wonderful.

Q:   *At that time, no one knew that the film carried an anti-colonialist message.*
A:   Columbia has forwarded me all the reviews, and it is . . . I would have been ashamed if I had written them myself. Full of praise. But there is one that describes this film as "imperialist." When I saw the restored copy, it was being shown at the Academy Theatre, the Goldwyn theatre—the same venue that was offered to Mrs. Goldwyn when Sam passed away—with a screen of twenty meters . . . what a feeling! Dawn Steel, the woman who runs Columbia, had shut down the studio to invite all the employees of Columbia to see the film. Half of them had never seen the film before—they were too young! Twenty-seven years old . . .

There were three hundred seats. When the curtain opened, I was thinking: "My God! How big is this screen!" I felt very reassured by what I was seeing on the screen. The last film shot in 70mm was *Ryan's Daughter*. *Doctor Zhivago* was shot in 35mm and was blown up to 70mm.

Q: *You have told me that you didn't look at the rushes during the shooting of Lawrence . . .*

A: You know, the rushes, it is fine. It is nice to see what the actors are doing. But if you know how to do your job well, and I very often keep an eye on the camera, then you know exactly what you are doing.

Q: *No surprises?*

A: Yes. Sometimes. Playing, for an actor, is all about thinking. If you think right, you walk right. Sometimes, with very immobile actors—and remember that stars have a sense of immobility—you are surprised by the force of thought. Kate Hepburn called that "horse power." You know, recently I have been working with alcoholics who were nearly paralyzed and whose look and immobility were extraordinarily powerful. This is something you can't always assess on the film set. I remember on *Pygmalion* (from the play by G. B. Shaw) I had cast Leslie Howard in the lead role. (I really liked him. He was a very nice person, very clever.) And in the scene with the seduction of the Devil, if Leslie was aware that I was going to zoom in on him, he wouldn't move. A couple of times, looking at him on the film set, I was thinking, "He goes too far with his immobility." And when I was shown the rushes, I saw that he was right. I didn't have to cut anything in his shots. But when I shoot, I usually know what surrounds me, what is on my left, on my right, and I know how the camera works.

Q: Lawrence of Arabia *has been printed in London, hasn't it?*

A: Yes, in Technicolor.

Q: *How did you choose Peter O'Toole for the role?*

A: We had discussed the possibility of casting Brando—we had offered him the job—but he wasn't available. He would have been very interesting. Nowadays, one says Peter O'Toole was born for the role. But Brando would have been goddamn interesting. The character could have been more mysterious . . . So, it wouldn't have been such a bizarre choice. But my first choice was Albert Finney. He was very young, and we conducted a four-day test with him. Eventually, after these four days, he didn't want the role anymore. He said he didn't want to be a star; of course I didn't believe him. What probably happened is that Sam Spiegel offered him a contract for eight films if he had signed on for *Lawrence of Arabia*. (He didn't tell me this, but this is what I think.) I was obviously disappointed and worried as we didn't have any actor for *Lawrence*. I started to spend all of my days in the cinema watching as many films as possible. I was going from one cinema to the other, everywhere in London. I don't know how many I saw. And one day I saw a film called *The Day They Robbed the Bank of England*, and there was this actor playing a B role.

And I looked at him . . . interesting face, good actor, and I told myself: "There he is." On my way back, I contacted him. I had never seen him on stage, at Stratford, where he used to play. Apparently, he had played a great Shylock, one that Robert Bolt had seen. So we did a day of testing and, as we had no time, we dressed him up as an Arab. He was marvellous, interesting. Today, they say Peter O'Toole was born for the role. But . . .

Q:    *However, he does not look like (T. E. Lawrence) . . .*
A:    You know, if you look at some photos by Lowell Thomas, the journalist who made Lawrence famous, sometimes there is a certain likeness . . . Of course, Peter is more beautiful, taller, but I thought that if the film was good and if Peter was good, nobody would notice it after five minutes. And this is what happened. The truth is that none of this is of any importance. If you want to perform the role of Mrs. Thatcher, it is harder because everybody has seen her on television. But in twenty-five years, it will be easier.

Q:    *And the other roles?*
A:    Alec Guinness—I have always admired him. And when I saw this film again someone who was sitting next to me asked, "Who is this wonderful actor who plays Prince Feisel?" That was Alec Guinness. He is very good.

Q:    *Omar Sharif too.*
A:    Of course! He is fantastic! He came out of a mirage to become a star!

Q:    Lawrence of Arabia *has changed the life of all these people!*
A:    Yes. But after this they have been under contract (with Sam Spiegel) for quite a long time.

Q:    *This is bizarre, you talk about Spiegel with warmth despite the fact he robbed you!*
A:    I knew he had been in prison once, but I learnt later that he had been in jail three times! I don't know how he landed on his feet every time! I never asked him. Unlike Robert Bolt, I have some affection for these pirates. Sam was one of them. However, he had a lot of charm. He took some huge risks to obtain certain things. He would never fall back. If tomorrow we had to make a film together and I needed the main street of Madrid, Sam would personally go to meet the King or the Prime Minister and would obtain it. And the following day he would say: "Baby, I am so sorry, we only have it for four hours!"

Q:    *How long did it take to film* Lawrence?
A:    I can't remember. It was long. Today's version is shorter than the original one by a few minutes. I had to cut a couple of things. For reasons I don't know, all those scenes that we had originally shot have lost their sound track. We had

to do the voices again. Omar came in for a recording session, Peter too. Alec was recorded in America along with Arthur Kennedy and Anthony Quinn. But Jack Hawkins died. And there is a full scene where Jack turns around and faces the camera, and we tried to synchronize his voice with that of another actor. A three-minute scene. And, in the end, we decided to cut it off, as it wasn't corresponding. The lip movement did not work. I didn't want the public, after learning about our reconstruction work, to notice this. Moreover, from the perspective of the drama's continuity, we could allow ourselves the cut. It is a pity as the scene contained one of Bolt's favourite lines. When Allenby says, "I am a gardening sort of a general." This is a scene where he flatters Lawrence . . . as he has just seen some blood on Lawrence's back.

Q:   *Has your conception of the character of Lawrence evolved?*
A:   I think that twenty-seven years ago our vision had started from a good point of view. Of course, there are many people who criticise the film from an historical perspective. We have tried not to make it sensational, and I think it is pretty close to the truth.

Q:   *Have you met any of the witnesses?*
A:   No. I talked a lot about Lawrence with Robert Graves. They knew each other. Graves had a pretty distant vision of Lawrence, almost humoristic. At that time, he was in the hospital where I was going to meet him. He was very nice man, very funny. He was saying: "Lawrence was a fascinating guy, I liked him a lot, a lot! But you can't believe everything he says. Some stories are true, of course, but others, honestly. . . . "

Q:   *O'Toole told me that he had met some Arabs who had known Lawrence.*
A:   Well . . . A lot of people claim having met El Aurens! At that time, they were all young, all these boys, and obviously they have all seen him from afar! I don't believe it.

Q:   *Are you conscious that you were responsible for creating a legend?*
A:   No. Lawrence did it.

Q:   *He was half forgotten when you did the film.*
A:   Yes, of course. We have only resurrected him.

Q:   *You did more.*
A:   Ha, ha, ha!

Q:   *The film is epic . . .*
A:   This is true. When I saw it recently, the people were asking, "What do you think of it?" I answered that I found it excellent! All of this is so far removed

from me! I know I made it but I have the feeling it doesn't have anything to do with me anymore! The critics were often very harsh with the film when it was released. I remember Penelope Gilliatt, in one of the Sunday papers—this was very funny—she added "the two and half pillars of wisdom" to the title. This wasn't wrong in relation to the book! For instance, we were asked why we decided to show Lawrence learning how to ride a camel? I say, "Why not?" "Because he has learnt to do it years before." "That's true. But isn't it more interesting to show him learning to ride while also discovering the world of the desert?" This is a liberty one takes with the truth, but I don't have the feeling that I committed a sin! If we had shown him riding like an expert from the very beginning, the same critics would have asked us, "Why?"

Q:   *Steven Spielberg admires the film.*
A:   Yes, I know.

Q:   *Me too.*
A:   You will certainly like it even more. This afternoon, I was actually telling this to my correspondent in New York, Robert Harris, the author of this remastered *Lawrence*. I asked, "Is it doing well?" and he told me that the film is successful and that the film holds up very well. Except that generally we turned the sound up too loud. Too bad. But why is *Lawrence* a success today? This is wonderful, but why? Robert Harris told me it is because of the quality. New York, Washington, everywhere. They had a hard time in America to check the quality of the projections at each of the venues. There are even some who installed 70mm projectors specifically to see the film. This is miraculous. What strikes me is the dialogue of the film. Nowadays, there is no dialogue like this anymore. Sharp, short, moving. This is more moving than I could remember.

Q:   *How did you meet Robert Bolt?*
A:   This was his first film. I had worked with a charming writer on *The Bridge on the River Kwai*, Michael Wilson, who has passed away, and who had been blacklisted by McCarthy. [Producer] Sam Spiegel and I decided to entrust the scenario of *Lawrence* to him. He worked on it a little while, but the result was awful. I had met Bolt and asked him if he would write a test-scene. About six pages. They were fantastic. I told Sam, "You see the difference?" "Yes." That was it. This is how we hired Robert. Who, I must admit, was very suspicious about us cinema people. He was from the theatre. He had also been a school teacher.

Q:   *He was very much on the left too.*
A:   Absolutely! This explains his suspicion towards all this money. Moreover, he had been arrested in the middle of the writing *Lawrence*! He had lain down in the street.

Q:    *Lain down in the street?*

A:    During an anti-nuclear demonstration. He was arrested with Bertrand Russell! A distinguished arrest . . . Robert was sent to prison.

Q:    *Was he on the set during the shooting?*

A:    A little. I am not sure he came to Spain. Yes, he came during the shooting! He came to Spain! He is even in the film. I put him in a shot where you see him staring out a window at the end before the intermission. When Allenby convinces Lawrence to go back to the desert, Lawrence is on his own after Allenby wishes him good luck. There are a lot of people looking out the window at Lawrence. The officers look down at him and the one in the middle is Robert Bolt. He looks very young. He smokes a pipe and is standing by a little fountain. I love working with him. We know each other so well. The writing of *Nostromo*, that we have just finished, has been a real pleasure.

Q:    *When will you shoot?*

A:    By the end of this year. We were meant to shoot this summer but the release of *Lawrence* has postponed everything.

Q:    *Have you finished casting?*

A:    We have cast one part, but the delay . . . We need new actors. I wished I had Paul Scofield, but he couldn't wait . . .

Q:    *Who are you thinking about now?*

A:    I don't know. I have some interesting ideas. However . . . The main character of *Nostromo* is strange, very bitter, in his sixties. At the end, you learn that he has been tortured, and he broke up, he gave some names away . . . But the characters are so surprising! Mrs. Gould, a young miss twenty-three years old, English; her husband, thirty-two; Monihan, the most spectacular, sixty . . . there is a super-nasty South-American, Montero, a very beautiful role. There is also an old Italian man, with two daughters, one is seventeen, the other twenty . . . and Nostromo . . . a very strange film. Conrad at the end of his life wanted to transform *Nostromo* into an opera. Truthfully it is nearly an opera . . . Many people are being considered for the position of the cameraman. I wanted Vittorio Storaro, but he cannot because he will be doing the next film for (Bernardo) Bertolucci . . . *Nostromo* needs very dark shadows, very bright lights—the characters are bigger than life . . .

Q:    *Isn't it surprising that you, a son of an English accountant, are so interested in films that are big adventures?*

A:    I have never forgotten the first time I saw a movie. I was fifteen or sixteen and my dad forbade me to go to the cinema. And I have never forgotten the sensations I felt to see some other places on the screen. I recall the film *Mare Nostrum* [1925] by Rex Ingram. This was his first film shot in the Nice studios. Very recently, I was discussing this with Kevin Brownlow, and he brought me a tape of the extracts of the film. A wonder! There was a wonderful scene where Alice Terry, the spouse of Ingram, was shot . . . Excellent! I think this is this film, this feeling that brought me to travel. I will never forget the first time I saw the Mediterranean Sea. And the train! Why do I love these trains so much? There will be some in *Nostromo* . . . My dad and mom were divorced, and my dad, with an extreme kindness, took me with my brother on the Rhine.

Q:   *In which year was this?*

A:   I was born in 1908, so I was about fourteen. Just after the war. We went to Switzerland, then on the Mediterranean Sea. What a shock! The sea! The sea! I remember writing him a letter shortly before his death and I thanked him for making me travel. It was extraordinary at that time. You know, my dad was a certified accountant, very able—he could add four columns of numbers just by looking at them. And he left my mother for another woman. I think he developed a form of culpability that he carried with him for the rest of his life. My brother was his favourite. I was the fool. My brother became the boss of the international services of the BBC. He had written two novels before he turned twenty-one. He became a journalist—a brilliant one. We don't have a lot in common. He went to Oxford and my dad told me, "Frankly, you are not worth the trouble of sending you there." I believed that it was true. I was very close to my mother. She had an artistic temper. Her family name was Tangye and she was from Cornwall. Her entire family had worked in the tin mines. My maternal grandfather was also an inventor and his brother was Sir Richard Tangye. They worked with Brunel, the engineer who constructed the first tunnel under the Thames . . .

Q:   *He also had submitted a project to build a tunnel under the English Channel before doing business in Africa . . .*

A:   . . . Really? But he drowned himself in the end. He built bridges, buildings, everything. In short, Brunel created a boat, the Great Eastern, with a frame made of iron, and he couldn't launch it into water. This became a joke throughout the entire country. After a couple of weeks, my two grandfathers arrived with a hydraulic jack, they built a quite few of them, and were able to get the boat into the water. They said: "We have launched the Great Eastern, and the Great Eastern has launched us." I knew grandfather very little. He moved to Birmingham where he started to manufacture pumps, Tangye pumps. Then, eventually, Tangye engines. I don't know why but you don't hear about these people anymore. They have been forgotten. They *were* famous though.

Q:   *And on the side of your father?*
A:   My paternal grandfather was an institutor. A line of institutors. I am certain that I inherited my temper from the Tangyes. Some French blood, probably. So I started to dream about big adventures. I still dream of them.

# David Lean: The Legend of the Century

## MICHEL SPECTOR / 1 9 8 9

As THE LEADER of postwar British cinema with *Brief Encounter* he quickly became an undisputed master of the big screen. Despite the prestige and acclaim of his epic films, they lacked neither lyricism nor emotion. The works throughout his impressive career include *The Bridge on the River Kwai*, *Doctor Zhivago*, and the famed *Lawrence of Arabia*, whose most recent version, restored and lengthened, will be screened at this year's Cannes Festival and released on May 17. We had the chance to sit down with David Lean.

Standing at six-foot two and with sixteen films to his credit, eighty-year-old Sir David Lean is a monument. His confident and rigid posture resembles more that of an army officer. He speaks slowly and deliberately in his distinguished, noticeably British accent. Thrilled with the U.S. reception of *Lawrence of Arabia*, which he considers his best work, the English filmmaker has now returned to London after a thirty-year absence.

It was there in 1927 when Lean first became involved in film. He started off small, first as a "tea boy" and then as a gopher at Gaumont Pictures. By 1932 he was quickly becoming one of the most sought after film editors in the industry. In 1942 he took his first steps to becoming a director, thanks to the king of the London stage, Noel Coward, who hired Lean as codirector for *In Which We Serve* (which he would later brilliantly adapt into other forms). The film was critically acclaimed and the public immediately recognized Lean as being at the forefront of British cinema. In 1946, *Brief Encounter* brought him even greater notoriety, despite shocking English audiences with its principal theme (adultery). Today, his movie still serves as a textbook reference in film schools for editing and construction.

---

Originally published in *Studio Magazine* (no. 26, 1989). Translated from the French by Sargon de Jesus.

In later years, Lean's adaptations of Dickens classics would show another side of the director—a side that would earn him both the condescension of cinema traditionalists as well as his international fame. *Great Expectations* and *Oliver Twist* demonstrate a true sense of image and composition, a strong affinity for dark romanticism and the beautiful strength of emotion, which became Lean's trademark in his spectacular films thereafter.

In effect, in 1957, *The Bridge on the River Kwai* is the first of his ambitious and renowned films which, through its unexpected setting, seemed to relate the tale of the century. It was lyrical, though somewhat paradoxically it also showed restraint. His critics would label him an academic. History would prove the film a classic. Lean's movies made their way around the world and left a mark on generations. *The Bridge on the River Kwai* was followed by *Lawrence of Arabia* and *Doctor Zhivago*. Those three films alone garnered nineteen Oscars—a record.

A fourteen-year dry spell separated *Ryan's Daughter* and *A Passage to India*, his most recent film in 1985. During that intervening period he worked on a host of projects that were never completed, among which were a project devoted to Gandhi and another to the mutiny on the Bounty.

The rerelease of *Lawrence of Arabia* (a longer, restored version) will be prescreened at the Cannes Film Festival and will be distributed worldwide, given its success in the United States.

Still, David Lean longs to tackle another film. This time it is an adaptation of Joseph Conrad's novel *Nostromo*. With the support of French producer Serge Silberman, production should begin soon. The story follows an adventurer who died along with the secret of a hidden treasure—a treasure that cost him his life.

STUDIO:    *What happened after* Lawrence of Arabia *came out in 1962?*

DAVID LEAN:    Over the years, I myself cut out twelve minutes. Then Sam Spiegel and others—I don't know who because no one has ever told me—cut approximately another half hour. Two Americans, Bob Harris and Jim Payneton then proposed editing the film to recover the original version.[1] It was very difficult since the original reels had been lost. Shepperton Studios in England, where we archived the film, had changed ownership twice. The soundtrack, the dialogue, the music, special effects—somehow everything was destroyed. Lord knows how that happened. Bob Harris and Jim Payneton retrieved the pieces from around the world by recovering various copies that had also been damaged. They brought everything back to the Goldwyn Studios in Los Angeles where I came to help them. We went to see some of my old friends at the MGM lab who recovered the negatives and made copies for us in 70mm. We had to be very careful. You can imagine that after twenty-six years certain scenes were in very poor condition. They then used the only soundtrack still in existence to make a new digital recording in six-track Dolby Stereo. Now the sound is more powerful; the copies are more refined. I think that the end result is better than the original film! The movie now runs three hours and thirty-six minutes. It's still missing about four minutes, but we've recovered nearly everything.

STUDIO:    *How did you feel about working on your movie more than twenty-five years after it was shot?*
DAVID LEAN:    It's very odd! I had the impression that the movie had nothing to do with me anymore. It's so old that it feels like another life. But at the same time, I know full well that it is my movie, and I am very happy that it can be rereleased. Typically, the lifespan of a movie is but a few weeks.

STUDIO:    *It's also a throwback to your first profession as editor . . .*
DAVID LEAN:    That's true. But back then I worked with my editor at the time, Anne Coates, who I believe is the niece of Arthur Rank, of the famed gong.

STUDIO:    *At the '88 Cannes Festival, the British film industry honored you . . .*
DAVID LEAN:    That poor English cinema. I had the feeling it really doesn't exist! In England, the establishment always scorned the film industry. Unlike other countries, the state never helped us. We never received any support, financial or otherwise, to encourage shooting in England. Look at the studios: they're all empty. It's really a shame because I find that for such a small country we have contributed more than our share to the development of cinema. Chaplin, Hitchcock, Olivier. Just those three . . .

STUDIO:    *Do you consider yourself an English filmmaker?*
DAVID LEAN:    I am an English filmmaker. Of course. It's sad that in England if you make the "big" movies, people become wary of you. Especially critics. Sour grapes, perhaps. Aside from *The Last Emperor*, no one wants to put money into big productions. For *Kwai*, *Lawrence*, *Zhivago*, and *Ryan's Daughter*, I never thought to look for money in England. I knew that they would have given me nothing. It was the Americans who invested in the movies, and it was they who made the money. *Doctor Zhivago* earned me more money than all of my other movies combined.

STUDIO:    *Is that why you left England?*
DAVID LEAN:    I left England because of the taxes! I was levied a 98 percent tax while one of my wives also claimed another share. When I went to meet with the tax collector, he demanded a colossal amount. What else could I do?

My accountant recommended I leave the country for a year to avoid being charged taxes. So I left, which was terribly difficult. At the end of that year, I think I was shooting *Kwai* and so I stayed abroad. I stayed there for thirty years and I have just returned to England now. I am a good, tax-paying contributor. And, thank the Lord, Miss Thatcher has cut taxes.

STUDIO:    *Do you agree with critics who separate your English phase on one hand, and then your American career on the other?*

DAVID LEAN:    The majority of people in England did so as soon as I started making movies. For my part, I honestly think that *Lawrence of Arabia* is my best film. But critics have always said that you can't compare it with *Brief Encounter* (1945). Granted, the two films have two very different styles.

STUDIO:    *You also have a reputation of choosing image over dialogue.*

DAVID LEAN:    Not at all. I found it very interesting watching *Lawrence of Arabia* again because I had worked with Robert Bolt, and that had been our first project together. It's wonderful now to hear such literary dialogue, which is absolutely brilliant. You don't see that in movies today. Classic lines are no longer in style. "Classic" may not be the right word. Let's just call it "literary dialogue."

STUDIO:    *It seems that all of the American filmmakers of Spielberg's generation consider you a sort of fatherly spiritual guide.*

DAVID LEAN:    I met Spielberg four or five years ago on a Concorde at the London airport. We recognized each other, got up, and shook hands. We made the trip together, and he told me that he had deliberately copied certain small things from some of my films, which flattered me, of course. Since then, we've remained friends. As for Martin Scorsese, he actually helped with the production of restoring *Lawrence of Arabia*.

STUDIO:    *Spielberg was also going to produce your next movie,* Nostromo . . .

DAVID LEAN:    It is terribly, terribly difficult to find enough money in the United States since so few people have read the book. I find it rather tough to read myself. In fact, I suggest starting off at page 170 in the pocket edition . . . But everything seems to have worked out since a French producer came to the rescue [*that would be Serge Silberman*]. I wrote the screenplay with Christopher Hampton, the author of the play and then screenplay of *Dangerous Liaisons*. I'd like to shoot in Mexico or Spain.

STUDIO:    *What kind of movie would you like to make that you haven't already produced?*

DAVID LEAN:    That won't ever happen, but I would like to do a film on the movie industry and to do a musical. I want to do movies that I'd like to go see as an audience member. I would love to do a movie on the beginning years of Hollywood, when stars were really stars and the whole world enjoyed making films. Now that idea has probably failed by virtue of my mentioning it. I would still like to tell the story of one of those old producers.

STUDIO:    *What about the musical?*
DAVID LEAN:    I dream about having done it. What was the title again? I'm starting to go crazy. *An American in Paris.* There—something along those lines.

STUDIO:    *Music has always played an important role in your movies . . .*
DAVID LEAN:    Let me explain it to you. I always participate in the writing of the screenplay, and I always give directions for the music. When it should begin, when it stops, what it should express. When the composer starts getting involved—you'd think I was married to Maurice Jarre[2]—I show him the script. I talk with him, I tell him the mood of the movie, and very often I'll call upon him to rescue me because I've messed it all up. He'll ask why, and then I tell him, "Here we need to have a dramatic feeling and it's simply not there. You can do it with the music." People always think that doing a movie is like writing a book. All it takes is to sit down in front of a blank page and that you have all the time in the world. As a director, my problem is that I constantly hear the sound of dollar bills flying off. You have to work very, very quickly, and you can make huge mistakes. Or you might forget things. Music helps fix those lapses.

STUDIO:    *Nevertheless, when you've started shooting, everything is rigidly set to the music!*
DAVID LEAN:    I don't believe in improvisation. I don't believe that you can change a scene at the last minute, except for the smallest of details . . . I don't think that a truly great artist, a great musician, like Beethoven, could improvise. It's meticulous work. I have always said that making a film is like taking a picture, just one moment in time. There is a negative, and we try to develop it. In my soul, it's very clear, on all levels. When making a film, we try to shoot a positive from the negative. So we try to hire the actor who corresponds best to the character we have in mind. That's very difficult. We rarely ever get that. The actor may correspond 70 percent or 80 percent, seldom greater, to the character you've imagined. Then you look for a cameraman, you work on the set, and you are always under financial pressure. You want to shoot a scene under a bright sun and then fog moves in. How many days are you going to wait until you get that sun? Not very many. You have to then think about how best to redo the scene with the fog. And that positive that you're developing starts

to drift away from the negative you had in mind. Now that's how you truly make a movie. You have to pass through a net of various talents: a filter, if you prefer. If the director of the shot had an idea of what the film should have been and you disagree with him. You simply say: "It's too bright, too pretty. I want something more somber, less alive." Or you tell the actors: "Listen, this man is not the one you're playing! He has no sense of humor and the audience has to hate him." But actors don't like playing characters that the audience won't like. So we have to pass through a large number of filters in order to get to the final product. When I'm on the set, when the camera is up high in a crane, I always get the impression that I'm trying to write with a pen with a very, very small tip, but at the same time there's a two-ton truck behind me pushing me to write. It's too heavy, too demanding, but it's our job.

STUDIO:    *So you don't have a very good reputation when it comes to actors?*

DAVID LEAN:    I've said some regrettable things, a bit like Hitchcock, who is always quoted for having compared actors to cattle. I don't actually think he said that. As for me, I say that certain actors can be annoying and certain actors are really annoying once they are on set. You know, they can make a lot of fuss over everything, but that's exactly what they are: a bunch of bores. I enjoy working with really good actors. Someone like Katharine Hepburn, for example.[3] During rehearsals you tell her, "Try to act a little more ironic, a bit more sentimental, or a little more this or that." She does it. Like a beautiful instrument. She has wonderful technique. I don't suppose we'll ever work together again. I would have also liked to work with Celia Johnson[4] but she has passed away. One of the actors with whom I truly enjoyed working with is still William Holden.[5] A true pleasure. Not a single problem. In fact, it's the second-rate actors who are the most annoying. The stars are easy. I always say that if you're a young violinist and you need some help, you'd do better to go see Yehudi Menuhin.

STUDIO:    *Did you intend to be a movie director?*

DAVID LEAN:    No, certainly not. That's the difference between yesterday and today. If someone had asked me when I was young what I wanted to be, I would have said "assistant cameraman." And by "assistant," I meant to say the guy who carries a big camera on his shoulder and stays sitting on a crate while everyone else eats their lunch. Never would I have answered, "I want to be a director." I never even thought I could be one someday. Honestly. Today, it would be better not to ask that question to young people working in the business. They all want to be directors. Well, good luck. Me, I took it one step at a time, and I became an editor. I had a certain reputation in England. I became a sort of "film doctor." People called on me to stitch together the pieces of a movie. Little by little, I was offered a transition into directing and possibly the wisest thing I have ever done, I believe, was to refuse. I knew that if I didn't have the money, the actors, the screenplay, the cameraman, I was done for. I knew what they absolutely were not going to say: he didn't have a good set designer, good setting, or good actors. But instead they'd say: what a bad director. So I waited and waited. I received some very tempting offers while I was an editor. Finally Noel Coward[6] came to me. He was preparing to direct *In Which We Serve* (1942), and he asked among his friends who was the best cinema technician. Apparently, many of his friends gave him my name, and he asked me to codirect the movie with him. Americans have always been wonderful for my career. Everything I learned about editing, I learned from Merrill White, who worked on several Lubitsch films. I really had a stroke of luck to get to work with him. The American directors were really good to me. And of course, I did the movie with Katherine Hepburn, which was a wonderful experience. She is my best friend. I can still remember telling her one day, while were shooting in Venice, "Kate, I just got a message from Sam Spiegel who wants me to direct a story about prisoners of war." (*that would naturally be* The Bridge on the River Kwai) She said to me, "Take it. You will learn a lot from him and he'll learn a lot from you." That's how I got started with Sam.

STUDIO:    *So what did you learn?*

DAVID LEAN:    A new outlook. A new way of thinking. If you consider *Lawrence of Arabia*, it's a huge gamble that needs nerves of steel. Typically American, don't you think? Take Douglas Fairbanks Sr., for example. In my youth, before the Second World War, the American film industry was always a presence. And it churned out some great producers: the Goldwyns, Selznick, Louis B. Mayer, and Harry Cohn. I knew them, for the most part. Diamonds in the rough. And lots of guts.

STUDIO:    *You've produced very few yourself . . .*

DAVID LEAN:    I produced *The Sound Barrier* (1952) with Alexander Korda.[7] That movie was one I came up with and eventually I produced. I remember him asking me, "Who makes the final call on casting?" "I do," I answered. "Who approves the final screenplay?" "I do." "Who approves the final editing?" "I do." Then he asked me "So are you the producer?" And right then and there he gave me the role of producer, which was very generous on his part. Alexander Korda shot *Marius* (1931) in France, and then he came to England to produce *The Private Life of Henry VIII* (1933), which was a worldwide success. As he got older, he grew tired of producing. I always used to ask him, "Alex, why don't you direct anymore?" He would tell me that it was like going back down the mine shaft. He meant the studios, of course. Suddenly the doors close and then you're in the dark.

STUDIO:    *Have you experienced that yourself?*
DAVID LEAN:    Not really. I love it, you see. To me, making a movie is like being reborn.

STUDIO:    *So you want to go back down in the mine shaft?*
DAVID LEAN:    I haven't been down in the mine for a long time. That is to say in a studio in the way that Alex Korda meant. But when I get older, and I'm already pretty old, I suppose I would be willing to go back down the mine shaft to work on a few movies in the studio.

## *Notes*

1. See the article on the history of *Lawrence of Arabia* in *Studio* issue no. 25.

2. Maurice Jarre was awarded an Oscar for the music in *Lawrence of Arabia*. He went on to compose the music for the remainder of David Lean's films and won Oscars again for *Doctor Zhivago* (1965) and *A Passage to India* (1984). He is now working on the music for *Nostromo*.

3. Katherine Hepburn was the lead actress in *Summertime* (1955), directed by David Lean and which she considers one of her best films.

4. An English comedienne with roots in the theatre, Celia Johnson (1908–1982) was the star of *In Which We Serve* (1942) and *Brief Encounter* (1945).

5. William Holden (1918–1981) is one of the lead actors in *The Bridge on the River Kwai*.

6. Sir Noel Coward (1899–1973) was an infallible genius. Playwright, author, screenwriter, producer, director, and actor. This incomparable character from the English scene offered David Lean, the editor, the opportunity to codirect *In Which We Serve*, whose soundtrack Coward himself had written. Lean went on to bring three more of Coward's works to the silver screen: *This Happy Breed* (1944), *Blithe Spirit* (1944), and most notably *Brief Encounter*, also coproduced and adapted by Noel Coward.

7. Sir Alexander Korda (1893–1956). Director and producer from Hungarian roots, who became a naturalized Englishman in 1931. He directed *The Private Life of Don Juan* (1934), *Rembrandt* (1936), *The Hamilton Woman* (1941) . . . In *The Private Life of Henry VIII* (1933) with Charles Laughton, he became the very first English producer. From *The Thief of Bagdad* to *The Jungle Book* and *The Tales of Hoffman* to *Richard III*, his accomplishments as a producer manage to outshine his outstanding directorial career.

# Interview with David Lean

## KEVIN BROWNLOW / 1990

*In 1990, Kevin Brownlow began a series of lengthy interviews with David Lean for a forthcoming book on Lean's life. These interviews ran for many hours and crisscrossed the whole of Lean's life and career. Transcribed from Brownlow's portable tape recorder, they exceeded over six hundred pages. They are also considered the last interviews Lean gave before passing away in April of 1991.*

*At my request, and with unparalleled generosity, Mr. Brownlow offered them to me to condense down and include in this collection. They are, I hope, a thorough summation on Lean's life and work and will offer additional insights not found in the rest of this collection. Predictably, editing six hundred pages down to these few is not an easy task, and one has to take many liberties. Therefore, any lapses of logic or confusion in the narrative can only be attributed to me and not Mr. Brownlow.*

*—Steven Organ*

KB: *Because of your Quaker upbringing you were not allowed to go to the cinema until you were much older. What did you imagine it was like before you actually saw it?*

DL: Well, you know, I got a jolly good picture of it, and then I broke the laws and went and saw things. And the more I saw, the more I was bitten. I was swimming in waters that were completely familiar and pleasant to me.

I always feel at home behind a movie camera. I really do. There are horrible moments, of course, when you don't know what to do or an actor is playing it up, but on the whole, I've had a wonderful time with my hand on a movie camera. I just love it and I feel at home. It's my friend.

---

From interviews conducted 1990–1991. Previously unpublished. Edited by Steven Organ. Published with the permission of Kevin Brownlow and the David Lean Estate.

I had an uncle Clement and he had a wife, Edith, and they both liked me very much. On my tenth or eleventh birthday they gave me a Kodak Brownie box camera. In those days it was an enormous compliment. It was the first time somebody had given me something which made me feel special. And I found that I could take rather good pictures—it was a sort of secret of mine that I had, that I felt I could do this.

I'll never forget going to the Gaumont Studios in Shepherds Bush—that's where I first started in the movies—and I went into the camera department on my first day. There was a Bell & Howell camera on a bench. I said to whomever was there, "What has this photographed?" They said, "The last thing it photographed was *Roses of Picardy*." And I remember putting my hand out and touching it. A sort of sensual pleasure; awe. So I just loved cameras. Still do.

KB:  *Do you look back in your childhood with pleasure or do you look back on it and think, "Thank God that's over?"*

DL:  No. I have a very clever younger brother who was three years younger than me. There were just the two of us, and I was an absolute dud. And I remember my father saying to me, "Look, I'm sending Edward up to Oxford, but, to be quite frank, you not worth it."

KB:  *He actually said that to you?*

DL:  Oh, yes. And I agreed with him. I was absolutely convinced that I wasn't worth anything. And it's been a damned thing, really. Because, do you know, Kevin, I've never had any fun out of my success. I've never enjoyed it. I've always thought this is some sort of luck, trick, fluke that's happened to come my way. I've had a lot of fun in the movies, but the fun's been more working with other people than doing what I thought was any good.

KB:  *How did* Brief Encounter *develop out of Noel Coward's* Still Life*?*

DL:  I wanted to do something else after *Blithe Spirit,* and I said to Noel, "I'd like to try something different." I was very keen at the time—we all were, we'd formed a company called Cineguild, Anthony Havelock-Allan, Ronald Neame, and myself—and we were all very keen on a book called *The Gay Galliard* which was about Mary Queen of Scots. I said, "I'd rather like to try something like that." And he said, "My dear, what do you know about costumes? You know nothing. You don't even know how people walk. Look, stick to contemporary scene and stick to what you know. Don't be foolish. Here, I tell you what, I've got this sketch, have a go at that." And he said, "I'll write you a script very quickly." And he went away and within two days had a full script of *Still Life.*

I read it and he said, "Well, what do you think?" I said, "Noel, I don't think that it's any good. This woman arrives at a railway station and gets some soot in her eye, meets this man, and they arrange to meet next Thursday, and it goes on and in the end they part. It's got no surprises in it. It's not intriguing. You're not saying to the audience, 'Watch carefully. This is interesting.'" And under pressure I said, "Well, supposing we started with a fairly busy waiting room. There are two people sitting at a table talking. A man and a woman. Into the door comes another woman who's a dolly and sits down at the table and you follow them. And as she sits talking you realize that there's something not quite right going on, and a train comes into the station. 'That's your train,' says the woman. 'Yes,' says the man, 'I must go. Goodbye.' He shakes hands with the other woman, and then you go back and explain that this is the last time they see each other. They were never going to see each other again. And you play the first scene in the picture—it made no sense to you at all and you didn't hear half the dialogue—again, and at the end of the film, with an added piece, perhaps, with the husband." He said, "Say no more," and off he went, for about four days, and he came back with what was essentially *Brief Encounter*.

KB:   *Who thought up the name Cineguild?*
DL:   I think Anthony Havelock-Allan. I was the director, Ronnie was the cameraman, and Tony was the producer for Noel Coward because Noel wasn't really interested. Tony ran the show. I said to the two of them "Let's split everything a third." And we did that. Even now, Tony and Ronnie get a third of *Brief Encounter*. Money still comes into me from *Brief Encounter* and I get money out of *Great Expectations* and *Oliver Twist*.

One day they came to me and said they'd like to leave. I won't go into the story, but they left to make films on their own because they thought that I was sort of highbrow and would only make respectable art films, which never make any money. They went off and made these other films.

KB:   *Such as?*
DL:   Well, I remember Tony went off with Valeria Hobson and did a film called *Blanche Fury*. I think Mark Allergret directed it. Ronnie did a series of films which were quite successful. And my first film outside of them was *Summertime*.

KB:   *Tell me about* Summertime?
DL:   Ilya Lopert, who was an art house distributor for a man called Robert Dowling, came to me with a play by Arthur Laurents called *The Time of the Cuckoo*. And I said. "Look, I think we can turn this into a successful film, and I think we might be able to have Katharine Hepburn for it." And sure enough, they produced Kate. I don't know how they did it, but Kate and I made this film together.

I rewrote a lot of it. I worked with Arthur Laurents for some time, and when the film was finished, I said, "Well, what did you think of it?" He hated it, of course. He said, "Very pretty." But it was quite a success at the time. In fact, I remember I got a cable from Kate Hepburn saying, "You made a smash. Love, Kate." Very sweet of her. I never did make another film with her, unfortunately.

KB:    *What sort of person is Kate Hepburn?*

DL:    Oh, she's wonderful. She's one of these electric personalities. I've never met anybody quite like Kate. She was a pleasure to work with. She had tremendous courage. I always admire the courage that some of these big stars have. I mean, she's got a scene where she's holding a sixteen millimeter camera and she's walking backwards and falls over the edge of the canal into the water. You try to walk backwards while holding a camera to your eye and fall backwards into a canal; it take a lot of courage and she did it first time off. Wonderful.

A lot of *Summertime* take place in a pensione. It's supposed to be on the Grand Canal, and we built a pensione in a sort of square on the Grand Canal. I remember Kate had a scene where she was walking across the terrace on this set and during rehearsal she tripped over a loose tile. I thought, "Oh damn, what a nuisance." And I said, "Let's do one more." She tripped again. I went and examined the tile and there was no loose tile at all; it was just her tripping to show her nervousness of the situation. She could do that sort of thing. Slide things in like that that you would never dream were invented.

KB:    *Prior to* Summertime *you also adapted two Dickens novels. How were you selected or did you select it?*

DL:    Well, you see, I liked *Oliver Twist* very much. Always had. I'd only read two Dickens books.

KB:    *Which were they?*

DL:    *Oliver Twist.* And then *Great Expectations*, after seeing the stage show at the Rudolph Steiner Hall. I was terribly impressed by the production, and as I read the book I thought, "What a movie!" And that's what I did, and we got started working on it. I was actually so in awe of Dickens that we got the biggest expert on Dickens, Clemence Dane. A big woman, very intelligent, knew everything about Dickens. And I asked her would she do a script, and she said she would. I suppose it took about two months, maybe less. It had practically every scene in the book, but done in shorthand so one never got to grips with any one scene. It was appalling.

I remember saying to (producer) Ronald Neame, "Look, Ronnie, it's no bloody good." And he said, "Well, what are you going to do?" I said, "I'm going to have to do it all myself." What I did first was that I read the book without any other thought except will this make a good movie scene and left out everything that I thought wouldn't. You see, I got a sort of list. I got continuity with huge gaps in it. I said, "Now, we'll sit down and we'll link these up in some way." And that's just what we did. We linked up all the scenes I thought would make good movie scenes with efforts of our own. I'm not quite sure how we did it, but it worked and the scenes we used did us proud.

You've got to savor Dickens, you've got to enjoy it. You can't just skip through these massive great scenes with a sort of Dickens mystique hanging over them, it just doesn't work.

KB:    *So, after* Great Expectations *you directed another Dickens novel,* Oliver Twist. *How did that come about?*

DL:    I wanted to do another film after *Great Expectation* that was not based on Dickens. But I couldn't find anything. So, I said, "Right, well come on, it's not a serious crime. Let's go for *Oliver Twist.*"

Alec Guinness then came to me one day and he said, "I want to ask a favour of you." And I said, "Yes. What?" "I want to ask you for a part in *Oliver.*" I said, "Alec, there's no part for you in *Oliver.*" He said, "Well, there is you know. Fagin." I said, "Are you out of your mind?" Alec was about twenty-seven years old, and all I could see was the pale young gentleman. He said, "Look, I'll just ask you one thing: give a test. Don't come and look at me, look at the makeup. Don't come and look at the clothes, just let me appear on the test set." And that's what happened. He came on looking more or less not too far removed from what he looks like in the film. Of course I was bowled over by it and he got the part without another word.

KB:    *Had you had other people in mind prior to Alec's screen test?*

DL:    No. Look, God knows how many years ago it is. I don't think . . . I can't remember that we had, no. But once having seen it in that test we knew we were in business. He was just wonderful. And you see he hit it bang on. We had no difficulties in the shooting. Very pleasant. Unlike some of our other encounters.

KB:    *That brings up the issue of directing actors. How was it that you had absolutely no experience in stage work, yet you were able to cope with actors?*

DL:    It was terrifying. You see that's another thing about the cutting room. In the cutting room you are correcting, a lot of the time, mistakes in performances. You'll take a line, the sound track from take five and put it on the picture of take one. All sorts of fancy fakery like that. You'll cut to someone else's face when he or she gives a wrong intonation.

Working with Noel [Coward] was a tremendous thing for me because, I suppose later, I more or less copied him. On *In Which We Serve* I had a very nice cast, you know, very nice people, and I just found myself obeying my instincts and with a great heave of moral courage said what I thought to them. And most of the time they listened to me.

Anyhow, I gradually learnt. But one paid the price for it. I remember my biggest disaster with an actor was on the film I directed of Noel's play, *Blithe Spirit*. I got into a position where Rex Harrison wouldn't do something. He was being much too nice and his whole part in *Blithe Spirit* is that he snaps at his ex-wife and his present wife. You know, the character will turn around and say, "Oh, shut up!" And Rex was playing it "Oh, shut up, dear." Very sweetly. Because in those days, Rex liked being liked. And that is a failing of a whole lot of actors. They want to be liked by the audience.

So, I thought it was time I pulled Rex up on being too pleasant to both his wives, Connie Cummings and Kay Hammond. And I told him so. In the end he said, "Alright, we'll do another take." And we'd do another take, and it'd be exactly the same, which is an old acting trick with directors. You have to have a lot of courage to say, "No, it's exactly the same. Cut. Let's go again." And this happened and in the end we were looking at each other across the set with completely blank faces. Not one of us giving way. So I said, "Rex, I know you think I have no experience and am no good as a director, but I think I'm a bloody good cutter, and if you don't say and do what I say in this particular instance, I'll leave you in shreds on the floor." He did it the way I wanted.

KB:    *I noticed in the [television programme]* South Bank Show, *when you were doing* A Passage to India, *you give the actor the atmosphere. I've always thought that is one of the most valuable things you can do rather than tell them how to do a scene. How did you find out about that technique?*

DL:    I don't know, but you see film acting is in fact thinking. If somebody is running away from having murdered somebody, running down the street, and you have that small figure running away from the camera, if they're thinking correctly, they will run and walk correctly, because the thought dictates the walk. So I take a lot of trouble explaining to actors the atmosphere I'm trying to get. Then I talk to them about the situation they are in and gradually, hopefully, suggest to them what they're thinking. Most of the time that works.

I'm often amazed by the way actors come up to me at the end of the day and say, "I cannot thank you enough. You were so helpful. I've never had this before." And all I've done, it always turns out, is given them a little confidence and a kind of tour of the scene we were doing, and it helped them over the humps.

I'm told that many directors say almost nothing. I know that Willie Wyler used to drive actors mad by saying, "Cut, let's do it again," without giving any advice. I remember a story a friend of Willie's told me. After sixteen takes Willie finally said, "Let's all go to lunch." Willie saw the friend and said, "Wasn't that wonderful? She really got it on that last take." And the chap said to Willie, "Got what? I didn't see any difference between the first take and the last take. What so overjoyed you about it?" Willie said, "Well, you see none of the other takes had a flow and a rhythm. The others had hesitancies and all sorts of things which that last take hadn't got." The friend said to Willie, "But why didn't you tell her?" Willie said, "If she doesn't understand the flow of the scene, no amount of telling her will make her do it. It'll just happen. So I go on until it happens." Does that make sense to you?

KB:    *Yes, absolutely.*
DL:    I tend to talk far too much. I'll go up and find it very difficult not to talk about the flow or the turn or whatever it is. But Willie just went on.

KB:    *We've touched a little bit on the craft of editing. I was wondering what are your thoughts on disguising cuts. What did you think of Eisenstein who endeavored to make the cut crash?*
DL:    What did I think of that? Well, there's cuts and cuts, and cuts you can't disguise everything. You know, sometimes you want to shake people up and absolutely astound them by something that they don't ever expect to see. That's very exciting too. But it's always telling a story in pictures. I recently had a huge compliment from the technicians at the Metro Lab. They were the ones who printed the reissue of *Lawrence of Arabia*. They said to me—first I must explain things to people who don't know about the printing process. In the laboratory they see the rushes every day, and they hear no sound because the sound is sent somewhere else. So it is just pictures. And they said, "We always like your films because sitting there, and seeing them silent, we always know what's happening." That's nice, you know? It's all very simple really. Just telling a story in pictures. That's what I try to do.

KB:    *If I looked at one of your cutting copies, would there just be one splice or multiple?*
DL:    You would find the cutting copy absolutely filled with build up and patches where I've changed my mind.

    I'll tell you another thing that I didn't mention to you. Half the thing of cutting—it's like acting. It's a question of balance. If you make a long shot run for eight feet, it's heavier than a long shot running for six feet. I call that absolute balance and very often if you alter the length of the long shot you probably have to add something to the close-up. But it's cutting from or cutting to that creates this balance.

Now editing is, as I say, telling a story in pictures. I also have to decide what the audience sees and when. You may think this rather curious: up to now I've always waited until a film is finished before I attempt to cut it. I start at the first scene and I go on from there because if I do that I get the excitement of telling a story from the first sentence on the first page. So I think, "We never start with a long shot. Wait a minute, what would happen if I started with a close-up and disclosed the long shot a bit later? Let them into the situation by degrees." I go through this process shot-by-shot.

It's the putting together of an enormous jigsaw puzzle. And the audience should feel that there are not any cuts. I mean, a cut from you to a close-up of me, or a close-up of me and a door, that's a cut you should be unaware of. If somebody goes out and slams the door and you have two pictures of the door slamming then cut to the person watching, and the echo of the door slamming is over that close-up, you'll never know you made a cut. It's got to be as smooth as knife going through butter.

The person who taught me more than anybody was Merrill White. He was one of Ernst Lubitsch's cutters, and he knew all about smooth cuts. He used to say, "You can cut from anything to anything and make it smooth and the audience won't spot it." I remember Merrill catching me on one thing. I had a long shot where somebody goes to sit down in a chair. And as he is halfway, about three inches off the chair, I cut to a close-up for the final little "bumpf" of him sitting down. He said, "Why did you cut there?" knowing jolly well why I'd cut there. I said, "Because it made an extra smooth cut." He said, "Look, David, there's no reason to cut it there because it's not telling you anything. It's just making a smooth cut. And a smooth cut is not a good enough excuse to cut into a close-up. If you've got to cut into a close-up, we want to cut it into the close-up. I suggest it's after the first line of dialogue. He sits down in a long shot, you cut to the other man looking at him, cut back and you're in close-up and the man speaks." That's rather good because he sits down in the long shot, cut to the man watching, cut to the close-up, and you're off. Probably better than cutting on the actual movement, although it gives one great pleasure when one cuts on the movement. You learn those sort of things. You can cut almost anywhere and make it interesting.

KB:    *What technique do you use when you have a sequence and you suddenly cut to an extreme long shot—a static long shot—how do you know where to cut? How to sustain the rhythm? Do you have any technique for that or is it trial and error?*

DL:   No, I know. You see one of the great things of showing a story told in pictures [frames] is the timing and contrast of various shots. For example, a character says, "I'm sorry to tell you, she's dead." You don't use another close-up within a minute of the original close-up. Let the initial close-up have an impact of its own. The sheer size of it. "I'm sorry to tell you she's dead." Bonk. Huge close-up. Bang. If you had a lot of close-ups before it won't have any impact. It's contrast. So with a long shot it sort of works in reverse. So and so is dead and go to a close-up. Now it might be very effective to go close-up— one—two—three—long shot. It'll give you a kind of loneliness to the figure. You'll get the impact, but you've got to time it right. I'm doing it about right there when I said "dead," close-up, one, two, three, cut, long shot. That room will look terribly empty after that big close-up. All contrast and I can think of dozens examples of that.

KB:   *There is an internal rhythm to the sequence which tells you what frame to cut or is that frame found by going backwards and forwards in the—*
DL:   No, I never wander backwards and forwards. Did you remember the scene in *Lawrence*—

KB:   *Blowing out the match?*
DL:   Yes. What I did was this: He holds up the match and he goes [blows]. I had the first part of the blow noise come over Peter and the last half over the sunrise. So the blow noise carries from his close-up over to the long shot. He was still blowing on the long shot. If I'd had him blow out the match and after the noise had gone I cut to the long shot, it wouldn't have had the same effect.

KB:   *But you were also dictated by the fact the match goes out so you—*
DL:   No.

KB:   *No?*
DL:   The match doesn't get blown out. I wanted the sound to blow in the desert and if I didn't overlap it into the long shot, it wouldn't blow in. The whole thing is that Lawrence blows on the match and it blows in the desert. If you'd finished the noise of the blow, then cut, you don't blow in the desert. He's blown a match, and, oh, there's the desert.

   Now the next thing was when to bring the sun up. And I thought: blow, one, two, three, four, sun. So I would have my foot on the moviola and I'd go "blow" and press the pedal and the film would start running. One, two, three, four, put a chalk mark on the film, got it! So I have a strip of blank film with a chalk mark at the end of it. I then get the real scene and I find the place where the sun appears. First shot. First picture of the sun appearing and I put the cross opposite the sun appearing and I go back to the beginning. I cut the sunrise where I started to time it. I have one, two, three, four when I go forward and the sun comes up after four. That's how I did it.

KB:    *Since we are on the subject of* Lawrence, *did you know or did you ever encounter T. E. Lawrence in your life?*
DL:    No.

KB:    *Did you ever want to?*
DL:    You know, he was always kind of a hero of mine, I always thought he'd make a wonderful film. And (director) Alex Korda wanted to make it.

KB:    *Who did he have in mind to play Lawrence?*
DL:    Leslie Howard, he had Leslie in mind. And I don't know what happened but it never came off. And then after *River Kwai*, Sam Spiegel said, "Can you think of anything?" I said, "Yes, *Lawrence of Arabia*." He didn't know who Lawrence of Arabia was. Of course, no American did at that time. And that's how it was done.

At one time I was going to have Marlon Brando play the part of Lawrence. Brando looked bloody marvelous, and I think he would have been very interesting, completely different from Peter, you know, completely different. But he couldn't do it because he was doing *Mutiny on the Bounty*, I think. And then there was Monty Clift who was on about it all the time, but I didn't really think Monty could do it. I liked him very much, but I wasn't sure that he was 100 percent behind it.

Q:    *Didn't you also have Albert Finney?*
A:    Yes. It was most peculiar. We did four days of tests with Finney, and at the end Sam said to me, "Will you take him on? What do you feel about him?" I said, "Sam, to tell you the truth, I think I can just drag him through, but I cannot say more than that." And then Sam came to me the next day and said, "He's turned it down!"

So I went to Albert and I said, "Why have you turned this down?" He said, "I don't want to become a star and I think this may make me a star." "Why don't you want to become a star?" "Because I'm frightened about what it will do to me as a person." I said, "Well, I can't answer that, that's up to you. But professionally, if you become a star it'll just offer you the best parts going." In the end he turned it down.

KB:    *How did you eventually settle on Peter O'Toole?*
DL:    I started doing a round of London cinemas. I did three films a day, and on about the fourth or fifth day I went to Leicester Square and saw the film *The*

*Day They Robbed the Bank Of England.* I had never seen or heard of him, but there was Peter O'Toole dressed as a silly ass English trout fisherman. I was with an Indian friend of mine, called Doctor Rishi, and I said, "That's him. Got him." He said, "You're mad, you're joking." I said, "No, I'm not joking. I think he's got a wonderful face and he can act. He could be Lawrence."

I went back to Sam and I was terribly excited because I was absolutely certain that it would work. I went back to Sam and said, "Sam, I've got him." He looked gloomy and said, "What's his name?" "Peter O'Toole." And he said, "He's no good." I said, "What do you mean he's no good?" He said, "I tell you he's no good. I just know it."

After about another week, I said, "Well, Sam, what do you want to do, we haven't got Finney, we haven't got anybody else. I've picked Peter O'Toole who'll be wonderful. I want to do a test on him, and I think you'll see you're wrong." He was very gloomy about it, but we did the test and he was fine. Just one day's test after those four days with Finney, and I thought he worked wonderfully. And I said, "Look Sam, look at it, come on." So he said, "A little better than I thought," or words to that effect. "Well Sam," I said, "I think you're cooked because you've got nobody else." He suggested one or two Hollywood actors, I've forgotten who they were, but hopeless, hopeless, hopeless. In the end he finally had to agree.

When we were well into the picture, I found out from Peter what happened and why Sam didn't want him. Sam was shooting *Suddenly, Last Summer* with Monty Clift. And Monty Clift was liable to go off on drunken bouts making Sam very nervous. So Sam started looking around London to see who could come in and take over from Monty Clift. One of the people he tested for the job was Peter O'Toole. Now Sam . . . Who was directing *Suddenly Last Summer?*

KB:  *Was it Mankiewicz?*

DL:  Yes. Joe Mankiewicz. He was doing it and Joe was shooting. Sam was too lazy to go and do any testing. Not that he could, I mean, I don't think Sam could test anything. So he sent an assistant director to do the test and what happened was this: The assistant director had the camera, the microphones, and the sound crew, and he stood Peter up in front of the camera and said, "Turn and look to your left, look at me, then walk away from the camera and stop when I say, 'Stop.'" So Peter walked away from the camera and the man said, "Stop," and he stopped. He said, "Turn round again," and now was in full figure. Then he said, "Right, now walk towards me." And Peter walked towards him and he said, "Stop." Now Peter was in quite a big close shot. Then the assistant said, "Say something." Peter looked straight into the camera and said, "Mr. Spiegel, your son will never learn to play the violin." Cut! And that, of course, came out in the rushes. And was never forgiven. Good isn't it?

KB:    *Incidentally, did you have to do anything to Peter O'Toole in terms of contact lenses or hair to alter the look of him?*
DL:    No. I mean we just dyed his hair blonde, that's all. No special make up. One of the cleverest things in *Lawrence* I think—I'm not sure whose idea it was, probably John Box—as you know Peter is given these robes fairly early on when he's accepted by the Arabs, and then the rot starts to set in. He gets the sort of power mania. And what they did was they gradually changed the material of which his Arab clothes were made, and they made it thinner and thinner until it was just muslin. At the end he looked almost ghost-like because the clothes he was wearing were the exact copies of the rich silk he wore at the beginning but they were almost transparent. It gave a kind of faded look which worked a treat. Nobody ever spots it.

KB:    *Who did you have before you had Omar Sharif?*
DL:    Sam told me he'd got a wonderful French actor for the part. An actor, I don't know if you know him, Maurice Ronet. He was blue-eyed, and I put him in Arab dress for a test. It looked awful. I sent a message to Sam saying, "Look I can't use him. He can't walk like an Arab and he doesn't suit the clothes." Sam said, "Well I've signed him up for the picture." And I said, "I can't help it." And he had (signed him). Eventually Sam had to pay him the whole of his money to got rid of him.

KB:    *Good God. So how did you eventually get Sharif?*
DL:    Oh, well, I was desperate. I was down in Aqaba.

KB:    *When you say Aqaba?*
DL:    The real Aqaba, in Jordan, where King Hussein has a house which he let Sam and me have. I was desperate because I knew Ronet was no good. I had said to Sam, "Look, Sam, I need at least six real Arabs who can speak English. I don't mean that they should be wonderful actors, they can do the odd line here and there; not totally inexperienced. I really do need them, and I'll put them in various parts of the film." Sam said he'd been to Cairo and seen many people. "Where are they?" I asked. He had some postcard-size photographs, about twenty of them I suppose, and I went through these photographs when I was suddenly stopped by Omar's face. I said, "Who's this?" Sam said, well, he was once a big Egyptian film star. So I said, "He looks good. I want to see him." So they got him over from Cairo, and I was even more impressed when I met him. I did a test and I thought he was bloody good. I said, "Sam, that's it." Sam

engaged him, laid out the contract with Omar committed to a total of eight bloody pictures. And you know he fulfilled that contract. Right up until the end. What was the sequel to *Funny Girl*?

KB:     Funny Lady.

DL:     Yes. And that last picture (*The Night of the Generals*) he got paid peanuts. Sam and Columbia made a fortune on it because he was paid nothing.

KB:     *He played a German General.*

DL:     That's right. But I think that was quite a good part for him.

KB:     *It was a good part, but I just can't see an Egyptian playing a German General.*

DL:     And then I staggered everyone by saying, "I'll play him as Zhivago." It worked. And that was the first picture he got his proper money.

KB:     *How was he to work with?*

DL:     Wonderful! That's why I wanted him for Zhivago, because he'll take direction. We both liked each other and sort of spoke the same language. I knew I could get all sorts of things out of Omar, you know, what I call "tickling the talent." And Omar has got a jolly good screen personality.

KB:     *What about the organization of* Lawrence of Arabia? *It's just mind boggling to consider all the various elements that were needed.*

DL:     I remember Tony Quayle coming out—I think we were in Wadi Rum, which is quite a spectacular place—and we had a marvelous mob of those camels and horses and Bedouins. But if you've got a good producer—and Sam was a first-rate producer, a wonderful organizer. If you wanted the traffic stopped in Piccadilly for ten minutes at eleven o'clock on a certain day and have six tanks go down the middle of it, if anybody could get permission to do that Sam could. He certainly did the same with this Arab business. I mean Sam got Anthony Nutting to write a book about Lawrence solely to get public-ity about the name, Lawrence of Arabia, because Americans are slow to talk about people they haven't heard of. And by the time the film opened, they'd certainly heard of Lawrence of Arabia. It was that sort of thing that Sam was very good at.

KB:     Lawrence of Arabia *is a film about Arabs and Sam was Jewish. How did he cope with that?*

DL:     That's something I shall never know, but that's another remarkable side of Sam. To think that Sam took his yacht down through the Suez Canal and an-chored it off Aqaba, it's an extraordinary achievement in its day. He was jolly frightened, and he used to have me sleep in the same room with him down at Aqaba, but I don't blame him for being frightened. That was very courageous and jolly good, hats off to him for doing that sort of thing. I mean I got fed up working with him because I could never believe what he was saying, and he couldn't keep his hands out of my pockets. Yet we were a jolly good partnership, Sam and I, and it was a big regret of mine that we didn't go on together. If I had gone on with him, I wouldn't have made any money. I had a 50/50 share with Sam in *Lawrence of Arabia*, and I'm absolutely certain that it was at least fourteen years before I got my first cheque, because Sam told me that it was a flop in all but the big cities. I believed him like an idiot. He also cut the film down because he thought he'd get more money by putting it on television, and he thought that the total length would never be accepted by television. So, it was difficult working with Sam. Nevertheless, in those early days, I was very fond of him and we used to giggle together, which I always like very much.

KB:    *Where was Aqaba that you used in the film?*
DL:    That was in a part of Spain along the coast from Caballeros and it was a dirty river bed. John Box built that mostly out of cardboard cutouts, very, very simple. The chief thing was the gun pointing out to the sea.

KB:    *You mean that was a hanging miniature?*
DL:    No, it wasn't a miniature, it was actually real. We built the gun.

KB:    *No, I mean the background town.*
DL:    That was built out of flats. If you walked through, it looked ridiculous, but it worked, from the camera setup you see. I was very pleased with myself because I took my courage in both hands and I did the main attack in just one shot. We added inserts later, but the main attack was just one big panning shot. Started the music as the camera started to pan and it worked. Looked jolly good when I saw it the other day, I thought.

KB:    *So where was the main location?*
DL:    Well, we started in June, and I went out there and I flew all over the place with a very nice English pilot called Jock Dalgliesh. King Hussein, who was very good to us, put him onto us. Jock knew the desert backwards, and he flew me all over the place. We used to land on mud flats, very exciting.

KB:    *What was the plane?*
DL:    Oh, a small thing like de Havilland Dove or something like that, may have been smaller. It was a de Havilland plane anyhow. We used to go looking for the various locations in this plane. And Jock would say, "Look down," on these vast mud flats and say we were going to land there. That's how we found, for instance, the place where we shot Omar coming out of a mirage. As soon

as we landed, everything was shimmering, and that's how we found that location. That was Jock. That's really how we made the film.

The really sad thing about the picture was that before we started shooting I'd chosen all the main locations, including the big desert locations. I left the best locations for the second half of the picture. Then, after we'd been shooting six months, Sam said, "I've got to go back." Sam tricked me, you see. I was in Paris with Sam and I was about to leave for Beirut and then fly on to Oman and start choosing locations, that sort of thing. I'd already chosen most of them, and I talked to Sam before leaving and something in the air made me terribly suspicious. I said, "Sam, as you know, we've only got the first half of the script, and I have a feeling you're tricking me into starting shooting with only part of the script written." And he said, "Baby, how could you suggest such a thing?" "Well, I'm suggesting it." And we talked for a whole day on this, and he swore on his mother's health, on everything he could cook up, and finally I said, "All right, Sam, I have to believe you." And I left for Beirut. I got up there, and within two weeks the actors were sent out and he'd done me. I'd been right the first time.

KB:    *How did you find out?*

DL:    Well, you don't send actors out if you not proposing to shoot. Expensive commodities. And so it sounds mad but that forces you to shoot, because what do you say to them, go home? You can't. So I started shooting, and Sam promised me that we'd have a break and we'd complete—Robert and I would complete the second half of the script. We knew vaguely where we were going mind you, but we hadn't got anything written down in any sort of firm form. And at the end—around about the end of the six months I think—Sam said, "Look, we've now got to finish the script." Now I don't know what he'd done, I don't know if he'd tricked the distributors, I don't know if Columbia knew anything about it or not, but after six months of shooting we were in so deep that very few companies would say, "Well, we'll junk it and make a loss," because we must have spent quite a bit. And I said, "Sam, you've cheated me; you'd done exactly what I thought." He said, "No, we've got to go to Spain for the interiors, this is the right time of year, and then we'll come out here again." I said, "I don't believe you." Of course, we never came out to Jordan again, and I never used those locations. Bloody shame. Robert (Bolt) and I had a plan for using Petra and now, of course, we couldn't. Robert had a marvelously glamorous idea of Lawrence riding in through the gorge, very narrow gorge with a dead, what's it called, like a gazelle, around his neck and throwing it to his Arab bodyguard, very good, very glamorous.

KB:    *And this was for political reasons that . . . ?*

DL:    I think—can't prove this at all and I may be quite wrong—but I would guess that there were lots of complaints about all this Jewish money, Jewish dollars, or whatever you'd like to put it, and it was very difficult at that time. It sounds funny now, but at that time it was a serious problem I think for Sam. That he could be accused of being a kind of traitor you know. I don't know how to put that better, but you get the rough idea. I've always guessed, and it's only a guess, that he was, as it were, forced with a very gentle velvet glove into the position, and we never returned to Jordan, never. And he swore we would do the rest of it in Spain. I knew Spain pretty well, and I said to Sam, "You go out and find it. Go out and find where I can shoot it, there's a lot of desert in the second half of the picture. And he said, "That's easy." And he started going off to various places with various people. And, of course, in the end he failed to find anything and said we must go to Morocco, which we did. The last part of the picture, with the blood bath scenes and all that, that was all done in Morocco. It's always been a regret to me because it could have been better, scenically, if we'd had in the end done the film in Jordan. And Sam didn't leave Jordan until he was bloody sure—or he thought he was sure—that he could do the rest in Spain.

KB:    *What struck me with the* Lawrence *script was how extraordinarily literate it was, that you simply do not hear very often such quality of dialogue. I found it terribly moving when O'Toole suddenly said, "The desert is an ocean in which no oar is dipped." When you were collaborating with Robert Bolt on that, what was your method of working with him, did he prepare it the day before?*
DL:    We used to talk. And the terribly difficult thing was to get rid of Sam Spiegel, because Sam, I've forgotten who he told but I think he said it in a magazine, that he thought his greatest contribution to a film was his work on the script. Now, honestly, without trying to be funny or mean or anything, his work on the script was a disaster. He used to make the most terrible suggestions, and Robert and I would look at each other when one of these suggestions came out because that would mean that the rest of the day was occupied in weaning Sam away from his ideas. He'd make terrible suggestions. I mean really ghastly suggestions.

KB:    *Freddy Young says that he would go in to see you in the morning and you would sometimes play the tapes of your talks with Robert Bolt.*
DL:    Oh yes. Robert is a wonderful reader of his own lines and you often read an exchange of dialogue that's he's written down and you've got it in type before you. I would say, "Robert, I don't understand this, what's this?" He'd say, "Let me read it," and he would read it, and it was just wonderful with his intonations. I would always say, "No more." Then, after a bit, it got to the

point where I got Robert to read the scripts as he wrote it, so we had Robert reading his own lines of dialogue. And I used to say, "Robert, anything you can think of, put it in. Say I see them lying down on the ground or I see them panting for breath, whatever it is. Add anything you like." But it was mostly dialogue. And Robert did this and hardly any of the actors would listen to it. Omar would, but nobody else. I think Peter might have listened to some of it, but the actors—I remember Alec wouldn't. Alec Guinness wouldn't come near it because they somehow feel that their creative ability has been taken away from them. I don't really know how that works because as the creation comes from the writer, I don't know why they should be worried about being faced by it, you see.

KB:    *Your reason for doing* Doctor Zhivago—*why did you want to do it?*

DL:    Well, Robert O'Brien, who was the president of MGM, wanted me to do *Zhivago*. Phil Kellogg, my agent, came to me and said, "David, there's this famous Russian novel that nobody seems to have read but lots of people enjoy. I've read it and I think it might be just wonderful for you, and Bob O'Brien thinks it might be wonderful for you. Please, please read it." And so I looked at it with its five hundred and something pages and I said, "Oh, God."

Now this was at a period when I was leaving Los Angeles, and I was going back to Europe to have a holiday. I took one of those great Italian ocean liners—the Leonardo or the Michelangelo—and we were crossing the south Atlantic and I said, "I've got to get down to read this bloody book." So I propped myself up and read all night. I read and read the first night and got more and more interested. The second night I thought, "I'll finish it tonight." I ended up sitting in my bed with a box of Kleenex by my right hand wiping the tears away. I was so touched by it. I thought, "If I can be touched like this sitting in a liner reading a book, I must be able to make a good touching film of this, with Lara and Yuri."

So, I landed wherever it was and I said, "Yes, I'll do *Zhivago*." And Bob O'Brien just let me have anything I wanted. I did the film and he did the most wonderful thing that's ever happened to me.

KB:    *I think you told me—the money?*

DL:    Did I? Yes, I got all—it made me a tremendous lot of money, and I think he told people not to cheat me. I owe a lot to Bob O'Brien and I owe a lot to *Zhivago*.

KB:    *Who took the role of producer on Zhivago? Who was the man who produced the rabbits out of the hat?*

DL:   Carlo Pointi was the producer of *Zhivago*, and he had a tie up with the man in charge of foreign sales who wanted Paul Newman as Zhivago. And Carlo Ponti wanted his wife, Sophia Loren, as Lara. I said, "Look, Carlo, if you can convince me that Sophia is a virgin, I'll play her, but she's got to appear that way." And I said, "Paul Newman I cannot see as Zhivago. I cannot see him as a poet, a great poet novelist." They said, "Well, you've got to see a film he's just made called *The Prize*." I went and saw the film and, although I admire Paul Newman very much as an actor—I think he is bloody good—I don't think it works. He works in certain roles you know. Miscast him and he can't overcome it.

It became very, very difficult, and we got to a sort of impasse. One evening I was in Madrid, and Bob O'Brien rang me up from New York and he said, "David, I've been hearing about your difficulties. I've had a talk to my people, and I want to tell you, you can cast whom you like, cast anybody you like, and I will accept them." I said, "Well, I would like to cast Julie Christie as Lara." He said, "Julie who?" "Julie Christie. You must see *Billy Liar* because that's where I saw her, walking down a street swinging a handbag and I thought, 'She's just delightful.'" I love Julie. She was bloody good in *Zhivago*.

KB:   *Can we talk about* Ryan's Daughter? *Why did you decide to shoot it in a manufactured village rather than a real one?*
DL:   Well, basically, because it's cheaper. Nearly every country in the world, if you put up a movie camera, you have crowds of people. And in places like Italy—I mean I did *Summertime* with Kate in Venice—the shopkeepers form a kind of blackmail ring, and as soon as you start acting they come out and clatter pans, shout, whistle, do everything they can to upset the shooting unless you pay them for their imagined loss of business. And so you are at the mercy of the locals. If you're working in real streets, you have to deal with public transport—you either have to pay quite a huge sum to the public transport people or take your luck with what you can get out of them.

So in *Ryan's Daughter* we did all sorts of things, you know. We built it all. In fact, we offered to leave the complete village set because with a little assistance it could have become a permanent feature. And they turned it down, there in Dingle, but they took on the schoolhouse set and made that real. And it still sits there. And it's one of the chief sources of income for Dingle now. People come to Dingle to see the schoolhouse set. They could have had the whole bloody village.

KB:   *Any particular reason you chose Dingle?*
DL:   Well, we were scouting for a location that had rough seas, that sort of thing. And I had two people who scouted for me. One up at the top in the

north and one at the bottom in the south, and we met at a halfway mark. They all took photographs, and I saw them and I thought, by far, the most exciting lot was the southern lot. And that's where we ended up doing it. And it's got some wonderful beaches—Inch beach, for instance—fantastic and some just wonderful scenery. And we just decided to do that, and then as a sort of intermediate spot between the beaches and other locations we put up the village inland a bit.

KB:    *The storm sequence is one of the best ever photographed. How did you come to shoot the storm scenes? Were those shot in Ireland?*

DL:    [Unfortunately] we ran out of weather because the days got shorter and shorter and shorter, and we hadn't got the storm. And I worked on three storms; we had three storms coming in and I did the essential long shots out of three storms. Then I left my assistant director, Roy Stevens, to do what I hadn't done. Second unit, you see. I gave him a complete list of shots, and we did a script in which he knew exactly what we had done. "I've done this, I've done that." He was to get "this, this, and that." We mapped this out between us—and so forth and so on. I also asked (production manager) Stephen Grimes to go to the Canary Islands and Eddie Fowlie to go to South Africa and . . .

KB:    *What had you known about those two places to give . . .*

DL:    Well, I'll tell you what we did, we thought of a place that was directly due south, that we didn't have to travel all over the world to reach.

KB:    *I don't understand. Why due south? What's the idea of it, what's the advantage?*

DL:    It's the quick way to the sun, isn't it? I mean, if you go west or east, you're going at a sideways angle, and you're gonna have X more hours flying time to get into the sun. So, Stephen Grimes went to the Canary Islands and, I think, they guarantee something like four days of beautiful sunlight per week. And so I said, "Alright, South Africa." So we got a charter plane, put tracks, lights, cameras, everything, and flew the whole bloody lot of us on one plane down to Johannesburg and then to Cape Town, where Eddie had found some lovely beaches. They looked just like the Irish beaches.

And that's what we did. We finished it off in, I think, two weeks.

KB:    *Still, the storm sequence that you shot in Ireland is very impressive. How did you work in those circumstances?*

DL:    It's bloody hard. I mean, these storms used to—they come in sort of gusts. You see, I don't know how far away, a mile away, two miles away, huge black clouds approaching, and it gets nearer and nearer. It's rather like the desert—a cold version of the desert. In Ireland, as the blackness comes, it starts to rain and within seconds the rain turns into hail, and the hail tears your cheeks to bits. We used to look at each other with blood running down our cheeks where the hail had cut us. Because when it comes in, it comes in I tell you!

KB:    *I know it does. I've been in it. But if it was damaging your cheeks, what was it doing to the lenses?*

DL:    Nothing because you—it doesn't go into the lenses. When I was on *In Which We Serve*, I was amazed by the wind. And on a military destroyer you have—I don't know what you call it, but in a car it's called a windscreen—it's a round piece of glass, optical glass, which revolves with a hole in the centre and as you turn the switch on, it goes round. And I thought, "My god, we could adopt this—adopt this for the camera." We built it. We got Panavision to build it. We used to put this up in front of the camera lens, turn on the switch and gradually this big piece of glass would get faster and faster and faster. And on the first exciting occasion we turned the camera on, I took a bucket full of water and threw it at the lens and within seconds it was clear, because of the speed of the glass going round. It's jolly good.

KB:    *But what about the lights? If you have lights in those conditions they usually explode, so how do you . . . ?*

DL:    Well, not if you cover them up. You know. Not if you stop the wet getting at them. And you can do that, you know. You put glass in front of them.

KB:    *And how did the actors take to the conditions?*

DL:    Well, it depends on the actor. I mean Leo McKern was just wonderful.

It's also very exciting. And I would go and do mad things—anybody will go and do mad things if they're excited. And it's very exciting when you start putting it all together again, putting it together, cutting the first close shots in with the long shots. The first time you see it working, you know, it's wonderful.

KB:    *Are there any other locations apart from Dingle and the foreign locations . . . ?*

DL:    That we shot in? Oh, lord, there was one place, where was it? It was about an hour away, where we worked on some great rocks that go down to the sea in great slabs. The thing I remember about that is working all day in the pouring rain and getting into my car at the end of the day, and as I put my hand on the steering wheel I felt a rush of water going down my sleeve—my elbows—about two to three inches of rain. You drive an hour, absolutely soaked, feeling very cold. But great fun, you know. Terrific.

KB:    *How do you feel about Ryan's Daughter, looking back on it?*

DL:    I think it's a much better picture—I think I'm right in saying this—I think it's a much better picture than the terrible notices it got. I mean, if, as you say, that's one of the best storms every photographed, I think that deserves quite a big mark in itself. I think there were some good performances. I think it was a good atmosphere. I don't think it was bad. I think lots of people now come to me and say how much they've enjoyed it—they've seen it on television or something—and I tell them about the notices, how awful they were, and they can't believe it. The critics, in some mysterious way, can become a pack; it's a kind of invisible contract between them all. So when you've reached a certain stage in your career, they literally hound you.

KB:    *Can we discuss the event at the Algonquin Hotel with the National Society of Film Critics? I met Richard Schickel . . .*

DL:    Oh really?

KB:    *Yes, and he was terribly upset at the quote in the [Stephen] Silverman book [David Lean and His Films] that had Schickel saying, "How could the director of* Brief Encounter *make such a piece of shit as* Ryan's Daughter.*" He said that he made mistakes when he was chairing that meeting, but he did not say that line and he would not have said it and he wants it conveyed to you that he was—it never crossed his mind because he is a great admirer of yours.*

DL:    This is not true, and I don't want to take it up again, so please don't. But I think—you see he did not chair that meeting, Pauline Kael chaired it. She took me in, holding me by the hand, and sat me at the head of the table. And Schickel did say that, and I think they were pretty well all pissed. I would not mistake (that comment), it really cut me to the heart, and it was Richard Schickel. No good taking it up and I don't want to start it again. I think he is a jolly good writer by the way.

KB:    *But, usually, when somebody writes something which has no validity, you brush it off because it isn't true. But you reacted to what they said as though it was gospel.*

DL:    You know when forty people burst out into print and tell you that it's a load of absolute rubbish, you tend to believe them. At least I do. Because when you finish a film, you are at your most vulnerable. Almost anybody could come to me at the end of a film and say, "I've just seen your film, why did you do this and that?" And I say, "Well, because of this . . . ." "Oh really, it didn't strike me in that way." And they can go on and the more they go on talking the more you believe they must be right. I don't quite understand it, but that's what happens.

Producers know all about that. So, when you've made a final cut, a producer can come in and say, "Look, that just doesn't hold up. I think you should cut it in half." And you find yourself agreeing with them because you are at your most insecure.

KB: *But even worse is the one that would say, "Wonderful. Congratulations." And go outside, shut the door, and say, "Well, that was shit."*

DL:    Yes, well, luckily I don't get that. I don't see it you know.

I think the trouble with me is that I'm—what's known as too commercial. I think with the highbrows I'm highly suspect. I'm too popular and the critics really act like a pack of wolves. In some curious way word gets around that "it's time we got hold of this chap and clobbered him." And they certainly did it with me in a big way. And in the end, after *Ryan's Daughter*, I didn't like going out to a restaurant because I thought that I'd be pointed out as the chap who did that disastrous, terrible, horrible film. I felt very ashamed . . . I didn't want to shoot another film. I thought, "What the hell am I doing if my work is as bad as all this? What am I doing? I'll do something else." And I traveled around the world, and I didn't make a film for, what, fourteen years? Just didn't make another film. I thought, "What's the point?"

KB: *But, during those fourteen years you were working very hard on* Mutiny on the Bounty, *weren't you?*

DL:    Yes, some of it, yes, for about two or three years. I also worked on *Gandhi* with Robert (Bolt) and then gave up because I thought we weren't getting a good enough script. If we were doing a film about Gandhi, it had to be more or less the bible. Simply wonderful.

KB: *And what about that documentary you made?*

DL:    Oh, well, Eddie Fowlie thought he'd found Cook's anchor—there was one of Cook's anchors, which was lost, and everybody tried to find it. He came to me one day and he said, "I think they've been looking in the wrong place." "All right," I said, "let's get Charlie Lahartel." Charlie was a Tahitian and also a diver. They went down to where Eddie thought it was located, and, sure enough, it was Cook's anchor. Eddie was right and everybody else was wrong. New Zealand television sent out a film crew, and we did a little documentary called *Lost and Found*. It's not terribly good.

KB: *You directed it?*

DL:    Yes, and I've got a copy of it somewhere. I ran it the other day. It was only shown in Australia and New Zealand, but nowhere else.

KB: *What's the latest on* Nostromo?

DL:    We're in. The money is being paid on the table today. The big issue is my insurance: $2.8 million to insure me. Fantastic, hmm? It's going to cost $43 million.

KB:    *Have you made any casting decisions?*

DL:    Not particularly, no.

KB:    *How many people have worked on the script?*

DL:    Have worked on it? Well, I've been a constant. And Christopher Hampton. The terrible thing is that Christopher got fed up with me. I don't blame him for it at all. He said in some magazine that he just dreaded the moment every time we'd get to a certain point I'd say, "Well now, we'd better go back to page one." He just dreaded it—all sorts of people I work with have dreaded it. As a matter of fact, I find that this is one of my biggest assets. I just plod and plod and plod away. And by the time you've gone through it, I don't know how many times all sorts of cats fall out of the bag.

KB:    *What made you want to do it?*

DL:    Robert (Bolt) had always talked about it. He said, "One day we must do *Nostromo.* I think it will make a wonderful film." And then Maggie (Unsworth) came to me and said, "Look, a lot of people have suggested *Nostromo* for you." Anyhow, I went in and had a go and I started with Christopher Hampton.

KB:    *Why did you start with Christopher when Robert Bolt wanted to do it?*

DL:    He wasn't there because he'd not written the script. He still had this terrible heart problem. Then one day, after Christopher and I had separated, I met Robert. Robert said, "How's the script? Can I read it?" And I said, like a rock dropping into mud, "Yes, of course!" Of course he started to spark right away, right away, and, because we know each other so well, we could kind of talk in shorthand. It means a lot to us, and we get along, and it's wonderful because I think that working together again has improved his disability. It's done something for his confidence, I think.

KB:    *When is it due to start shooting?*

DL:    January. But I think we could start—Maggie was saying to me just a couple of hours ago, "I think we could start a bit earlier and save yourself a bit of time." The thing I've had to do is to find the people who can take over from me if I keel over. It's all a very macabre business.

KB:    *One could understand. Doing a film is a bit like going to war. The preparations have to be very similar and you have to be physically ready to lead, right?*

DL:    I guess it is rather like that, yes. I guess it is. You do have a lot of officers and privates and god knows who else. . . . But you know, there really is no training for being a director. It's essential that you have a gift and, I suppose, if you have tremendous ambition, it's fairly easy to believe you have a gift when you haven't. I know quite a few people who have wanted to be a director—and have, in fact, become directors—because they like the *idea* of being a director. It sounds so glamorous. They think it's wonderful you can get tables in restaurants and that sort of thing. And I think one of the terrible dangers is ambition. I've never had it; I don't know why. Of all these things it's just a matter of luck. I've never thought to myself, "Oh, I'm going to be a great film director. I'm going to be a big film director." I've never thought of my career in those terms.

I've never really thought of being a film director. In fact, I've only just accepted, on a few occasions, thinking, "Well, I think you've been quite successful." I always tend to think it's because of my youth. That I was jolly lucky. Noel Coward used to say—talking about luck—"Fred Astaire lucky? Luck my foot!" And it's true, of course.

I'm pleased if something comes off, but my trouble has always been that I've never really enjoyed my fame because I thought it was some sort of fluke. And that's one of the great pleasures in seeing some of my old films. When I saw *Lawrence of Arabia* the other day, I looked at some of those scenes, I mean twenty-seven years old or whatever it was, and I thought, "That's bloody good."

# Appendix *Brief Encounter*

## DAVID LEAN

*In the fall of 1945, David Lean directed his fourth film,* Brief Encounter, *a film that generated a great deal of prestige to the British film industry by winning the critic's prize at the Canne's International Film Festival, as well as garnering Lean's first Academy Award nomination for Best Direction (the first British director of a British production to do so.) Although the film made back its initial investment, at the time of its release* Brief Encounter *was only moderately successful, never reaching the classification of "box office smash."*

*The following article, published in the* Penguin Film Review, *was written by David Lean shortly after the film's release. Though written almost as a defense for the film's "poor performance," Lean touches on a theme that will appear frequently in his interviews: the balance of creating popular, financially successful films while also being creative (and unconventional) in the art of filmmaking. Written over a half century ago, this article is far from outdated, providing opinions and examples that are even more relevant to today's business of filmmaking.*

*Because this article does not fall under this series' guidelines of being a formal interview, it is offered here as an addendum for the reader. It is, however, just as revealing as any interview Lean has given and offers the reader that rare opportunity to read a prominent filmmaker's unfiltered thoughts and opinions.*

*—Steven Organ*

*Brief Encounter* presents a problem. It has almost unanimous praise from the critics, both here and in America. At the Film Festival at Cannes an international body of film critics gave it an award for the best film shown at the exhibition. As films go, it was inexpensive, but *Brief Encounter* was not a big box-office success. Why? The answer is a considerable headache for every serious filmmaker, and I think this is a good opportunity to show some of our film-goers what we're up against—that is, if we're to stay in business, for films are made to make money, and they cost plenty. In terms of Wardour Street and Hollywood, big money-makers are automatically bad films. There is no such thing as a good film that does not make money.

The *New Yorker* says of *Brief Encounter*: "Noel Coward has expanded his short play *Still Life* into one of the most adult films in years. It is the story of an affair between a respectable British matron (Celia Johnson) and doctor (Trevor Howard)."

There comes the rub in two words: "adult" and "matron."

The great mass of film audiences are not adult, mentally or physically, and they are not very interested in adult problems. (It is almost unbelievable, but an analysis of one leading Hollywood film-actor's fan mail showed that 53 per cent of letters and postcards were from fans of under thirteen years of age; 43 per cent from thirteen to twenty-one, and only 4 per cent from fans of over twenty-one.) The greater proportion of film-goers are under twenty-one mentally or physically; they go to the movies as an escape from reality. The big movie executives know this, and have provided a liberal diet of saccharin and silver linings, which has rewarded them with enormous profits. This great audience also likes to associate itself with the characters on the screen; so the makers have provided characters which will satisfy this desire.

Just watch the various couples in any cinema when the big pictures comes on the screen. Let us take Bill and Mary, sitting in the back row of the stalls. Main titles and first sequence—a general settling down and lighting of cigarettes. Introduction of female star—Mary makes a comment on her general appearance and her clothes in particular. What she is *thinking* is whether this celluloid female is a worthy character for her to transfer herself to for the evening. Introduction of male star—no word from Bill, who is busy sizing up *his* champion for the evening. (Hollywood pays great attention to physique. A lot of the grooming process takes place in the gymnasium, where chest and muscles are developed. No young Romeo likes to associate himself with the puny and the weak.) Star meets star. They are quite obviously meant for one another, but male star is not yet well enough acquainted to make a direct approach—Bill can do better than that, and does. He puts his arm around Mary. The stars are dancing together—just like Bill and Mary at the Palais. The Palais is not quite so grand, and Bill and Mary are not *quite* so well dressed, but if things were a little different, they would be *just* like that. They have gone out onto the moonlit terrace overlooking the sparkling sea, and he is telling her that he loves her. The screen Bill is speaking for the real Bill and putting things rather better than the real Bill, *and* to the accompaniment of a vast orchestra. They kiss. Fade out. So do Bill and Mary, and when, after the performance has finished, Bill and Mary are walking home in the dark, there go Lana Turner and Van Johnson.

Long after Bill has married Mary, they *might* be interested in seeing the story of "a respectable British matron." But then they don't go to the cinema so often. They had their own home, and don't have to escape from Mum and Dad; and besides, there's that other film up the road with Betty Grable, Tyrone Power, four bands, and Technicolor. And life is very drab. I see their point.

Hollywood knows all this, and takes good care to satisfy the customer. When you next go to the movies and see a glamour girl waking up in the morning with every hair in place, don't imagine that this is a mistake on part of the director or continuity girl. It is part of an elaborate plan to give the audience what it wants. A shop girl earning three pounds a week doesn't pay to see an exact replica of herself on the screen—she pays to see what she would *like* to be, in looks, dress, and mode of living. Hollywood gives her what she wants, because Hollywood wants her money. Displease several million Marys and thousands of pounds are down the drain. The only criterion of success is box-office, and in the past any producer or director who, ignoring the dictates of well-proven box-office formulas, has set out to satisfy his own taste and convictions has indeed been a brave man.

And don't forget that Hollywood has produced several such men. Some have had box-office and prestige success, others have ended in commercial failure; but they have all been advanced spearheads in the development of the industry, and without them the cinema would either be dead or dying. Don't underrate the production centre which has produced such names as: D. W. Griffith (the first man to shoot close-ups, the first man to discover the dramatic use of cutting—long before the Russians, the maker of *The Birth of a Nation* and *Intolerance*); Eric von Stroheim (the director of one of the first big realist pictures, *Greed*; a box office failure which he followed with the box-office success, *The Merry Widow*. In an interview, he is alleged to have made the following comment: "When I saw how the censors mutilated my picture *Greed*, which I did really with my entire heart, I abandoned all my ideals to create real art pictures, and made pictures to order from then on. My film *The Merry Widow* proved that this kind of picture is liked by the public, but I am far from being proud of it, and I don't want to be identified at all with the so-called box-office attractions—when you ask me why do I do such pictures, I am not ashamed to tell you the true reason: only because I do not want my family to starve"); Charles Chaplin; Douglas Fairbanks (did you see the twenty-four-year-old *Robin Hood* at the New London Film Society show? In settings, speed, and sheer gusto it put most modern films to bed); Lubitsch (the first man to take the cumbersome talking apparatus and give it mobility in the first true screen musical, *The Love Parade*, no mean technical achievement); King Vidor (the director of *The Crowd* and the first all-negro film *Hallelujah*); Walt Disney (surely the most original movie-maker ever), and, latterly, Orson Welles, who in *Citizen Kane* took the sound and picture cameras and gave them a shaking from which they have only just recovered. The film wasn't a popular success, and Welles has now been tamed—temporarily; but his ideas have been adapted and used by almost all the big commercial directors and have had a greater influence on film technique than is generally supposed.

And that is the point. If *Citizen Kane* lost money, it was money that will be repaid in future films, for without these spearheads the movies will become sterile and die in a mire of played-out box-office formulas. I wish the film industry as a whole could provide funds for such men as Orson Welles to go on making financially risky experiments, for without them there is no future. *Citizen Kane* was a too-advanced spearhead. Audiences weren't ready for the shock tactics of sound, camera, and story-telling techniques; and, above all, they were not ready for the character-study of a man with whom they could not associate themselves. If Rosebud had been Betty Grable, things might have been different.

The outbreak of war in 1939 introduced an entirely new phase in the history of films in this country. The British public, starved of almost all the other forms of escapism, flocked into the cinemas, and picture grosses beat all previous records. *But* in their everyday lives the same audiences were being brought face to face with reality: the life-and-death reality of the blitz. They knew what it was like to be frightened, and they knew that death came with a whistle and a roar, not with fifty violins and a heavenly choir. The Hollywood romances didn't seem so convincing. The over-dressed stars were living in a dream world which had no connection with the reality of clothing coupons and blackout. But Hollywood was 6,000 miles away, and that was our chance—we took it with both hands. *London Can Take It, One of Our Aircraft Is Missing, In Which We Serve, Millions Like Us, The First of the Few, The Way Ahead*, and many others. The British audiences enjoyed these pictures. They were about people like themselves—people they understood. But, above all, they were so "real."

An exciting thing happened: the box-office receipts from British pictures started to go up. Within two years, British pictures on British screens were proving themselves serious rivals to the American product. The Hollywood

producers were not slow in answering the challenge, and soon sent over a series of war pictures to regain their supremacy. Their efforts were not rewarded
with the hoped-for success. It was almost unbelievable, but British pictures
were taking more money at the box-office than many of their American rivals.
And they still are—so far.

British films have got themselves into their present position on what audiences call their "reality." What they really mean is that the best British films
have integrity, a very different thing. If one were to put real life on the screen,
it would be deathly dull. Films are not real. They are dramatised reality. You
will be wondering why, in the light of all this, *Brief Encounter* did not "go" with
this great new and enlightened British audience. I think the answer is that in
this particular case we went too far; too far, that is, from a box-office point
of view. We defied all the rules of box-office success. There were no big-star
names. There was an unhappy ending to the main love-story. The film was
played in unglamorous surroundings. And the three leading characters were
approaching middle-age. A few years ago this would have been a recipe for
box-office disaster, but this wasn't the case with *Brief Encounter*. The film did
very well in this country in what are known as "the better-class halls," and
now it is having a similar success, but on a smaller scale, in New York. The
film was put on there at a small cinema called the Little Carnegie, and it has
had almost unanimous praise from the New York critics. I should like to quote
portions of *Newsweek's* review of the film. Under the heading, "Coward Shows
How Again," the critic writes:

> One of J. Arthur Rank's protean connections with the American movie
> industry is a new company called Prestige Pictures Inc. Under this label,
> some eight or ten of Rank's British films will be presented in the 1946/7
> season to American audiences, chiefly through the studio or art theatres
> of the larger cities. In other words, these films are presupposed to appeal
> only to the discriminating.
>
> Judging by *Brief Encounter*, the first Prestige offering, somebody has
> made a mistake. The mistake lies in thinking that American audiences
> in the neighbourhood theatres of the smallest towns would fail to react
> to the film's universal appeal and utter honesty. Produced and adapted
> by Noel Coward from one of his short plays, this is a film that should be
> seen, not once, but whenever you lose faith in the movie medium. As far
> as this country is concerned, there is not a "name" in the cast. The actors
> look like people rather than fan-magazine personalities . . . nothing hap-
> pens in the Hollywood sense . . . and the film's two principal players go
> so far beyond merely competent characterization that, if you cannot

identify yourself with either of them, you can at least regonise your next-door neighbour.

The film started its run at the Little Carnegie, and at the end of the first week the box-office receipts were more than satisfactory. But at the end of the fifth week's run came a big surprise. The takings for Saturday broke the box-office record for the house! That was the *fifth* Saturday, when, in the normal way, business would be expected to be dropping off. This state of affairs can only have come about by word-of-mouth recommendation from those who had seen the film. The latest development is that the film has been given a wider showing than had at first been thought possible. Dare we suppose that this is the thin end of a wedge? It is possible that the same thing is about to happen in America as happened in England during the war? Have the great American audiences had too much saccharin?

The spearhead of the new attack on the American market was Laurence Olivier's production of *Henry V*, which has just captured the record for the longest continuous run on Broadway—twenty weeks and still going. All this doesn't mean that British films have swept America by storm and that Hollywood is in a panic. The most that can be said is that British films are having a success in America which they have never had before. In Hollywood terms, it's not a big success. But it is, I hope, the thin end of that wedge. Once again, don't underestimate Hollywood. She has yet to fire her big guns, for during the war most of her best film directors have been in the services, and their latest films have yet to be shown, so look out for the names of Frank Capra, John Ford, William Wyler, George Stevens, and Garson Kanin. They are all brilliant picture-makers. They have all made pictures about real problems and real people, and if the public wants realism, they are more than capable of giving it to them.

But to return to England. Why was it that the stand of British films changes so much during the war? Pre-war, the procedure for making a film was roughly as follows: the producer or director would find a story he wished to make, and he would go to one of the big film-distributing organizations and ask them to finance it. The distributor would decide whether the story was good (i.e. good box-office). If he decided it was, he would then ask for the names of the proposed cast. If the cast did not include names that he considered to be box-office, he would turn down the proposition. If the producer or director had decided that no available star actor was suitable, he had two alternatives: to abandon the film or to miscast a star actor. Not wishing to starve, he would probably choose the second course, and the film would proceed. When the film was finished, the agonizing day would arrive when the distributor would see the rough-cut (the first assembly of the film in continuity), in order to make his cuts and suggestions. This was a nerve-racking experience, and having spent many years as a film editor, I have sat in on many such sessions. When the light went up at the end of the show, all eyes would turn to the man from Wardour Street. What was the verdict? You would be surprised. The distributor was virtually in charge of production, story, cast, and final presentation.

The change in this condition of affairs started to take place in 1940, and the story of how *In Which We Serve* came to be made will illustrate the point. Filippo Del Giudice, of the then small Two Cities Films, Limited, approached Noel Coward to make a film. Coward said that he wanted to try his hand at a picture about the Royal Navy, but that he would do it only on one condition— that he had complete control over story, casting, and production. Del Giudice agreed, but first had to find a percentage of the money, and the usual round began. A well-known American distributor was interested in the proposition, but the negotiations finally broke down on a question of star names (the film subsequently grossed $1,800,000 in America). He then approached a leading British distributor, and again the negotiations broke down on the same point. We started shooting the film on Two Cities' money, and for the first six weeks of production there was no distributor. One day, the late Sam Smith, of the British Lion Film Corporation, appeared at the studio. He said that the Royal Navy and Noel Coward were good enough for him, and the film was finally put out by his company. It proved a very sound investment. From that moment Del Giudice embarked upon the policy of leaving the creative side of film-making to the film-makers, and, with *In Which We Serve* behind him, he successfully fought off all the old Wardour Street controls, and the following films appeared: *The First of the Few, This Happy Breed, The Gentle Sex, The Way Ahead, Blithe Spirit, The Lamp Still Burns, The Way to the Stars,* and *Henry V.*

At the same time that this was taking place, two other film-makers had similar ideas: Michael Powell and Emeric Pressburger. They had just completed *49th Parallel* and *One of Our Aircraft Is Missing* (another box-office success which had been turned down as non-box-office by another big distributor). These two men approached J. Arthur Rank, and asked for financial backing and studio space to make the films they wanted to make in the way they wanted to make them. Rank agreed, and Independent Producers was formed. Under their company name of Archers, these two produced *The Silver Fleet, The Life and Death of Colonel Blimp, I Know Where I'm Going, A Matter of Life and Death,* and *Black Narcissus.* Other producer-directors joined the group: Frank Launder and Sidney Gilliat (Individual Pictures), who made *The Rake's Progress, I See a Dark Stranger,* and *Green for Danger;* Anthony Havelock-Allan,

Ronald Neame, and myself (Cineguild), who made *Brief Encounter* and *Great Expectations*; Ian Dalrymple (Wessex Film Productions), who is now preparing *A Woman in the Hall, Esther Waters,* and *Far from the Madding Crowd.*

J. Arthur Rank is often spoken of as an all-embracing monopolist who must be watched lest he crush the creative talents of the British film industry. Let the facts speak for themselves, and I doubt if any other group of film-makers anywhere in the world can claim as much freedom. We of Independent Pictures can make any subject we wish, with as much money as we think that subject should have spent on it. We can cast whatever actors we choose, and we have no interference at all in the way the film is made. No one sees the films until they are finished, and no cuts are made without the consent of the director or producer, and what's more, not one of us is bound by any form of contract. We are there because we want to be there.

Such is the enviable position of British film-makers today, and such are the conditions which have at last given our films a style and nationality of their own.

# INDEX